# One Woman's War

In memory of all innocent people who have lost their lives in war and violence.

For all those who have lost a loved one, who have been displaced, who have paid a personal price for violence and hatred enacted in their name.

This book was written in hope for peace and respect for the human rights of all women and men who live between the river and the sea.

D.M.

# One Woman's War

Essays written in war,
for peace

by Dana Mills
Introduced by Sally Abed

*Five Leaves Publications*
www.fiveleaves.co.uk

One Woman's War:
Essays written in war, for peace

*by Dana Mills*
*Introduced by Sally Abed*

Published in 2024 by Five Leaves Publications
14a Long Row, Swann's Yard, Nottingham NG1 2DH
www.fiveleaves.co.uk
www.fiveleavesbookshop.co.uk

ISBN 978-1-915434-15-9

All proceeds from this book go towards
Palestinian-Israeli solidarity work

Printed in Great Britain

# Contents

**Preface**                                                                        7

**Introduction by Sally Abed**                                                      11

**October:** Imagine a day in which everything                                      19
you believed in is shattered to pieces

**November:** There is no path to peace, peace is the path                          47

**December:** A Christmas wish from around the corner                               121
from a little town of Bethlehem

**January:** The battle and duty to hold on to hope                                 193

**About the Authors**                                                              217

# Preface

Dear Reader

Thank you for picking up this book. Even greater thanks if you consider buying it. All proceeds go towards Palestinian-Israeli solidarity work.

This book is a personal diary of my life, as an Israeli Jewish woman working in peacemaking civil society, during events that unfolded in Israel and Gaza in the autumn and winter of 2023, but also, much before that. This is a very personal diary. All opinions and thoughts here are my own. They shifted considerably, as you will see, in the process of writing. I started writing to understand—first and foremost for myself. In addition, I tried to communicate to friends and comrades abroad what is unfolding here in Israel–Palestine. This diary is written from my point of view, as an Israeli peace activist. I do not try to assume other points of view; mostly because I think it's impossible. My philosophical-theoretical education comes from critical theory and twentieth century continental philosophy, especially feminist theory, which sees our position in society as defining our narratives. This is true tenfold when one lives under apartheid, as I do, on the side that enacts inequality and violence on others. At the same time these essays are about my relationship with other people and collectives: Palestinian citizens of Israel, Palestinians in the West Bank and East Jerusalem, Palestinians in Gaza, and left-wing advocates internationally.

I consider myself a political theorist by training, a dancer by heart and an activist by necessity. This is by far the most personal and revealing book I have written. This is also a different kind of personal diary. I joined Peace Now, then Israel's foremost peace movement, in 1995 at the age of thirteen. I went through shifts and turns that brought me to pursue a DPhil at Oxford and live there for thirteen years. In 2021 I returned to work in civil society full time. My life is one of immense privilege and luck, and my choices arise from wanting to give back to the community which raised me and to right wrongs that structure my life. I worked in Peace Now, the movement that educated me, and served as its director, as well as in Gisha, an organisation that focuses on freedom of movement to and from Gaza. This is also the diary of an Israeli working in peacemaking as a vocational choice. It is also a diary of political shifts: from the optimism of my youth in the 1990s, through the collapse of the Oslo paradigm, and the search for a new way to reflect on peace as just peace, peace between equals who are free. It is also the diary of changes in our thinking, on the frontline of peacemaking in Israel–Palestine, from stressing the 1967 borders as the root of all evil, to recognition of the Nakba—the forcible displacement of Palestinians which is at the basis of founding Israel as a sovereign country, and how reconciliation and transitional justice can look from this recognition. The only way to find life in peace here for Palestinians and Israelis between the river and the sea is to recognise wrongs past and present and find political constructs that remedy them. The events that led to the unfolding of the war did not start on the 7th October. Context here is essential to understand the challenges for peacemaking.

I am very pleased that my friend and comrade, Sally Abed, agreed to write the introduction to this book. She is a leader in Standing Together, a movement of which I am proud to be a member, that does extraordinary solidarity work here on the ground. Her perspective is very different to mine. I always learn a lot from her.

When I started writing this blog, I could not imagine in my worst dreams that three months later, Israel would be deeply entrenched in Gaza, we'd be nearing 30,000 Palestinians killed by the Israeli army, famine and diseases would be rampant and we'd see devastation of a whole culture in front of our eyes. I did not think the Israeli government would abandon the Israeli hostages in Gaza and put its focus on revenge. I could not imagine so many internally displaced Israelis would be abandoned by their own government. If you are interested in these essays, and in Israel–Palestine, it is your duty to speak up. I have always believed oppression hurts both the oppressed and oppressor, who lose their humanity in putting ample resources into sustaining oppression. This is not an equal price paid by both sides, of course, yet my deep belief is that none of us can be free till all of us are free.

Ceasefire now. Free the hostages. Political resolution now.

In solidarity,
Dana Mills
Tel Aviv, 7th January 2024

# Introduction

Writing this introduction to *One Woman's War* I am thinking back and reflecting on the past few months in my life. When the events of 7th October unfolded it was a weird experience for me, as a Palestinian citizen of Israel. I never had to deal with, or to face, a very real traumatising experience for Jewish Israelis inflicted on them by Palestinians. I never had to understand a trauma of this magnitude enacted on Jewish Israelis. The dynamic between us, Palestinian citizens of Israel, and Jewish Israelis in Israel, is a hegemonic partnership; whereas the end goal is clear, so is its distance from the status quo. We are striving for equal co-leadership but it is clear who's the victim and who is marginalised in the present. I should add that I don't like this this division as it dismisses other struggles—mainly class, gender and race struggles within the Jewish society. But for me the demand to understand that the master is hurting was a very difficult thing to comprehend. There was a dissonance and very raw feelings and recognition invoked since 7th October. I understood immediately that we were going to have to deal with a hegemonic traumatised society. I remember at 12pm there was the first strike to Gaza and I said: they are going to erase Gaza. I remember that feeling and then I panicked because I understood there would be close to zero possibility for us, Palestinians, to talk about that with the Israeli public.

As a Palestinian citizen of Israel it is hard for me to contain this experience. I am Palestinian but I am also part of Israeli society, though the experience of Israeli Jews is foreign to me and always will be. I knew Israelis saw themselves as the "victim" and thought through this narrative. It was already a very challenging assumption to navigate even before 7th October. Now I had to accept it as a very real immediate victimhood, and I had dissonance: I had to evoke radical empathy with the Israeli Jewish side. I was worried I did not have that in me, as I also had a feeling of an existential threat and crisis as a Palestinian. At the same time, Israel's response was antagonising to me in a very real sense as a Palestinian. So how do I do this?

Before 7th October, containing and assuming responsibility for Israeli society was difficult but now it has become much harder. What made this experience more accessible to me and what helped me with that was the fact that I have colleagues and friends who have endured loss, real loss yet who also managed to acknowledge me. This was the thing that saved me. It was not this big thing, a grand narrative, but a very real life issue of friends who lost their cousins or their parents and it simplified this process for me. I got to experience the daily lives and experiences of Jewish Israelis, like those depicted in this book. That is the thing that helped me as a Palestinian; the very real human experience of Jewish Israelis which is easy to dismiss and discredit by the world due to the very obvious power imbalance between Palestinians and Israelis.

What is happening in Gaza is unfathomable. Many of my Israeli friends are still thinking about the experience of 7th October, and I understand that, but we are reaching 30,000

Palestinians killed by Israel, people are starving, sick, displaced…
How does recognising this cancel your experience as an Israeli?
It should not. Recognising these facts should never disappear,
especially when we know there are Israeli hostages still in Gaza
who are directly affected by the continuation of the Israeli assault.
I ask myself while seeing Israeli friends whose lives were halted
on the 7th October: How can you hold your trauma so loudly
while ignoring unfathomable atrocities? This can only be
explained by understanding that the Israeli public has been
convinced, methodologically and systematically told, that the
subjection of Palestinians under military rule, and their suffering,
is a necessity for Jews to exist on this land. What helps me is
having very real human connections. We, Palestinian citizens of
Israel, understand that we are not merely part of Israeli society.
We are tens of thousands of doctors who treated some of the
injured, tens of thousands of colleagues and peers and friends
who know someone who endured grief and death. We
experienced this human loss directly. That's the human
experience which is brought to you in this book. It's not only the
loss but processing the loss. Palestinian citizens of Israel have to
internalise, accept and respect the Jewish experience merely to
survive in our society. We are in a hegemonic society. This is not
always out of empathy but out of necessity. You do not have an
option not to process it as you cannot escape it. It becomes
empathy when it becomes a human connection. For me as an
activist who is surrounded by people close to me who were
impacted by 7th October and still managed to hold very radical
empathy towards me as a Palestinian was transformative.

I hate it when people say about Israel–Palestine: "it's

complicated". No, it is not complicated. It's clear what is righteous. It is clear what are the injustices that are occurring and have occurred in the past several decades against my people. It is clear what needs to happen so that everyone lives an independent and equal life. That is not complicated at all. It is also not complicated to talk about oppression. Israel has to stop controlling millions of people through its military violence. What is complicated is how we get from where we are today to this very simple truth. This process entails a lot of deep understanding of the public you want to convince. This is something that has been grossly ignored, especially when it comes to Israelis.

It is almost impossible to not morally lecture as a Palestinian towards Israelis, how do you meet a person in her emotional state to organise and make an impact, when they are overlooking, condoning or supporting genocidal declarations against your people? How do you do it? The only fact I know is that we have to find a way. My message would be that I know it's hard. We, Palestinians, are at a historic junction where we are finally receiving popular support, globally. For many decades we have been silenced, delegitimised and marginalised; we are finally winning the narrative. That is exactly where our responsibility starts to understand what needs to be done in Israel–Palestine. Is overlooking the Israeli human experience a conductive thing? Saying things like "go back to where you came from" or "fuck you" to our oppressor. Is it conductive? In many ways Palestinian citizens of Israel will have to make a bridge between the Palestinian collective and liberation movement to the Israeli human experience. Palestinian citizens of Israel have to lead the new left together with Jews, in an equal co-leadership that never existed before.

You are reading a book written by a woman who is living through a war. I am also a woman though my experience is very different. I dislike the flattening narrative through which all women are somehow connected and responsible for each other by virtue of being women. Sisterhood of that kind can only make sense when it is extended to Palestinian women. There are millions of women who have been impacted by being denied basic conditions to give birth; by experiencing period poverty while being made homeless after Israelis bombarded their homes and who are imprisoned without the right to trial. If we are speaking about women in war, let us talk about all women in war. The limited scope of the liberal Israeli psyche is hard for me to relate, but I also recognise it as one of the major limitations of the Israeli liberal camp that has grossly failed to enact real change within our society. There was a wide and very vocal campaign that accused the world of being silent in the face of sexual violence used against women in the Hamas attacks of the 7th October. Whereas clearly even after what Israeli women and men underwent in the Hamas attacks, these Israeli women did not extend their solidarity to women who suffer as their houses are demolished by the Israeli army. These Israeli women did not mention Palestinian women who gave birth in horrific circumstances due to Israeli direct assault on hospitals and health provisions. Either we are in solidarity with each other in earnest, when Israeli women are able to extend their sisterhoods to Palestinian women, including in Gaza, or we are not in solidarity. Demanding solidarity for only one group of women is not sisterhood but a cynical abuse of the feminist narrative.

At the same time, I truly believe that women have more emotional flexibility and ability to contain complexity than men, as well as higher emotional intelligence. We can navigate deep emotional challenges as women. So we, as women, have different stakes at this moment we are living through.

The book you are about to read is, as the title says, "one woman's war". It is one perspective of the human experience unfolding in Israel–Palestine. It is written by an Israeli-Jewish member of the movement in which I am a leader, Standing Together. All proceeds of this book will go towards the movement. We have continued to work jointly, Arab-Palestinian and Jews in Israel, acknowledging power dispersions while centring humanity, during these difficult months, and will continue to do so after the war ends. I hope you join us, in the words of the slogan we have chosen for ourselves: where there is struggle, there is hope.

Sally Abed
Haifa, 8th January 2024

# OCTOBER

Imagine a day in which everything
you believed in is shattered to pieces

## Thoughts from Tel Aviv

I returned home yesterday after watching the heinous and murderous attacks on 7th October unfold from London. I was there with my mother, we had both landed before it all kicked off, and decided to stay the course of our planned visit. I have to say it was incredibly hard for me to make that decision, but knowing my mother was with me and safe felt like something to hold on to for as long as I could.

On 7th October, Hamas entered civilian areas in the south of Israel, killed and abducted citizens, and destroyed entire communities, in what is now considered one of the biggest massacres in the region. The Israeli military reaction against Gaza didn't fail to arrive; since then and as I type the Israeli army has been indiscriminately bombing Gaza and has now called for eviction of citizens from the north of the Strip (they have nowhere to go) and to invade Gaza anew (Israel has anyway controlled all the crossings since its so called 'disengagement').

My family lives down south, in the kibbutz of Magen in Israel. They were under siege for two days. They are good lefties (not that right-wingers deserve to be victims of war crimes!) and have been deeply horrified by it all. They have lost their home and their community. Nothing that they had exists anymore. They have finally, thank god, been moved to a hotel and family elsewhere. Millions of Israelis have been displaced.

The state was absent when these horrors unfolded. Citizens

called for hours and no one from the security forces came. The illusion that Israel had a strong and functioning army is gone, and to be honest, the state itself is missing in action (pardon the very bad pun).

The community response has been extraordinary. Volunteering across the country for everything: for the displaced, for the reserve soldiers called in, all the things that the state isn't doing—are being done by citizens.

I am feeling so many emotions at once. I am devastated at the loss my community is experiencing, a loss that will take us a long time to process. I am equally frustrated and personally depressed by the response of the international left who were silent (or even jubilant!) when the extent of Hamas' actions unfolded. I'm the last person to use the Stand with Israel trope, and I acknowledge every day in my work disparities of power between occupier and occupied, but the feeling that many people I call comrades or even friends could not bring themselves to condemn war crimes or to even acknowledge them when done to Israelis made me deeply paranoid.

On the other hand, the kneejerk response against Gaza in Israel is horrifying and is unfolding to be one of the scariest I can recall. I have worked in defending human rights of Palestinians in Gaza for a while, and it scares me to think of the future of Gaza.

And yet I hold my government to account for its actions, and demand of it the same morality it is seeking to critique: not harming innocent civilians. adhering to the rule of law, international law and safeguarding human rights. The state of Israel and international law were both consequences of the Holocaust. If 'never again' is to mean something it is to stop all targeting of innocent civilians, anywhere, even by Jews.

Whereas I am sickened to my stomach by Israeli propaganda, I am equally saddened by the lack of empathy of so-called comrades who are still unable to see grief and loss for what they are.

The biggest challenge now is to hold on to hope. It was clear to me for a long time that we need a paradigm shift. What was presented as alternatives from left and right, both was not working and not adequate for the changing reality. I hold on to the hope that we can rebuild better, all of us, between the river and the sea (because it will be up to us to keep fighting for peace and justice in our homes) and to fight for humanity and human rights for all.

I will try and write here when I can—things are very unclear, as I wrote above, but thank you to all who expressed solidarity in so many ways, and let's kindle the faith for humanity to triumph.


14.10.2023


What is to be done? Reflections on
possible ways out of a never-ending war

Good morning from Tel Aviv and first, a heartfelt thank you to new followers reading this blog! I started it during COVID, when my father died and I was stuck alone in Oxford. Now life has changed a lot, but there are new crises to consider. Yesterday I wrote about how we got here to yet another attack on Gaza prompted by an unprecedented massacre of Israelis in the South. Now, I'll do my best to write a little bit about how things might unfold, and what we can do and (to my mind) should be doing.

So, Israel has been heavily bombarding Gaza for the past week. Gaza has been under closure for over seventeen years. It's in the depths of one of the most horrendous humanitarian crises in the world. Half of its population is under eighteen. The Hamas rule there has exacerbated and made desperate a terrible ongoing situation there. Now, Israel is claiming it is going to bring in ground forces and re-occupy Gaza. A few things about this: not only is this a deeply immoral act, contravening international law and violating human rights, it will be very dangerous for Israel which is already paying a hefty price for continuing occupation of the West Bank and for holding Gaza under siege for those seventeen years.

A friend, who like me defines herself as a radical lefty, was texting with me this week. We are all, in the human rights and peace community, deeply concerned for the well-being of Vivian Silver, a prominent peace activist abducted to Gaza. My friend, like me, somewhat cynical, was saying how she felt marching alongside these sixty-plus year old women in Women Wage Peace, shouting for peace (when we preferred to focus on the occupation). How right they were, my friend said. And indeed, whenever wars break out here, once again we need to talk about peace.

I gave a talk in the USA two weeks and what feels like a lifetime ago. I was described in my bio as a peace activist. I guess that is also who I am, so in that light, I'll try and map out a few scenarios and what we can do to get out of this mess, not enter another round like this, and actually advocate for peace.

A few basic facts (everything is contested here, but you

know...). Israel is currently occupying the West Bank and East Jerusalem, as well as the Gaza Strip, via the control of freedom of movement in all its crossings, apart from one border with Egypt. Israel is also a country struggling for its liberal democracy which has been in a deepening crisis, as you might have seen in forty-plus weeks of demonstrations, which among other things, created strong civil networks which allowed a response to be made to this war.

There are several solutions debated around what is to be done.

First and foremost, any path forward must centre returning abducted Israeli citizens from Gaza. I know several people who have been abducted and cannot try to imagine what they must be going through. This must be an immediate claim regardless of anything that happens after. But what after that? The 'classic' response is the two-state solution, based on the Oslo Accords. Israel withdrawing from the West Bank and East Jerusalem, Palestine governed by the Palestinian Authority, and both living side by side. This was the result of the Oslo Accords and hefty American influence. Now, American presidents try not to get too mixed up in politics here, and I doubt anyone would try to champion this solution. It involves evicting settlers (which, as I'll write later, I believe should be done) and also relying heavily on the PA (Palestinian Authority) which has lost legitimacy. I don't see this solution—in its classic iteration, at least—as being plausible right now.

The other solution debated is the one-state solution. This can go in different ways: either Jewish supremacy between the river and the sea, which I fear Israel is trying to achieve by occupying Gaza, but cannot be sustained without making Israel a complete pariah state and abandoning all façade of liberal democracy. Gone are the 'shared values' discussions with Europe and the US, gone are art and culture and science collaborations abroad, all we'll have will be settlers ruling the land via active ethnic cleansing—which has been ongoing anyway via policies of occupation. We become Russia.

The other one-state solution proposed is equal citizenship for all between the river and the sea. This, of course, sounds great, and I've had many well-meaning liberals abroad preaching to me over stylish dinners that *this* is what we should be working towards, including the right to return for Palestinians displaced in 1948. But, this is a big jump from two peoples killing each other's children, as we've seen this week. There is no infrastructure in place, there is no trust between these two peoples. So, if you're in Brooklyn or North London it might seem a good solution, but from within the depth of this little troubled piece of land it feels completely detached.

What is to be done, then? The first is recognition, and this goes both ways. Israelis have to recognise the right of return, and the fact that so many of their hinterlands were other peoples' homes less than a decade ago. The practical outcomes of this may vary, but at the very least, recognition is key for any reconciliation. Also, bear in mind the majority of people living in Gaza are refugees from the Nakba. But, and here is where I lose the radical left and remain pragmatic, Palestinians have to recognise Israelis, and that Israelis are here to stay.

I often wondered whether all these theoretical and abstract supporters of decolonisation actually thought of what that meant for us. Go back to where we came from? I have the choice between

Russia and Wales (I would go for Wales, despite the weather!). This land in the Mediterranean is our home too. We're stuck living together, Palestinians and Israelis, and will have to find some kind of solution, as none of us are going anywhere. We cannot forever live by our sword. My thoughts at this point are that probably we'll have to find some middle way solution: recognition of the Nakba (Palestinian displacement before and during 1948) and redistributive justice based on that recognition, returning some land occupied in 1967 from Israeli control, *but also* accountability, international guarantees and safeguards for the existence of Israel as a home for Jews, as a state in which Jews have enshrined legitimacy or protected with some practical safeguards. The politics of revenge will bring us nowhere. An eye for an eye makes the entire world blind. We are all here to stay and we need to figure out a way to live together—acknowledge wrongs in the past (yes, on both sides) but also look towards a better future.

You may think it is a bit detached to be reflecting about this now. But actually, the current status quo of avoiding a solution altogether cannot be sustained. Many of us have felt for a long time something bad is going to happen, we just didn't realise how bad. Many of us want to escape the never-ending circles of violence. I would like my friends' kids to have a different future than my present. I would like the people of Gaza to not live in fear. I would like all people who want to live in peace, away from politics of revenge and hate, to become the loudest voice, while of course demanding justice, but ultimately focusing on a better future for all.

A South African friend wrote to me and said the biggest battle we'd have to face was the battle for hope. Preserving personal relationships constantly put to trial by our governments, fighting for a just future, different from the present. I am praying to keep doing that and to have enough strength to do that.

Thank you for reading, once more!

20.10.2023

## A note on empathy

An Israeli friend in the US wrote to me recently that what Israelis and Palestinians need from the world is more empathy. I've felt that for a long time, and this round makes it even more explicit to me. I remembered over the past few days that when I lived in Oxford I had a conversation with a then-friend. It was during one of the Israeli operations in Gaza, I spoke to her about my cousins who live in a kibbutz in the south of Israel (it's one of the kibbutzim where terrorists tried to abduct and kill people, but luckily the awareness of the guard duty squad saved them by a miracle). I told her I was very worried about my family, as they had been in their shelters for days on end. Her response was "people in Gaza don't have a shelter". She knew my politics and I confided in her in a moment of loneliness and worry yet this was what she had to offer to me. There are so many wrong things in hindsight about this response: first, surely you should hope not for more shelters but for fewer bombs? But more profoundly, it became apparent to me that she wasn't able to think about what it is like to be me. Not even a bit.

I'm going to explore two points about empathy and the current events in Israel/Palestine. First, I have been thinking about the boundaries of empathy and how hard, or impossible, it is to acknowledge them. Second, to think about what we can do to transcend those obstacles.

I'm going to make a claim that might feel controversial to some of you. First, I want to say, none of you know what it's like to live in Gaza. I say this because I don't know either, and there are boundaries to how we might imagine human corpses and worlds that were shattered. We can't imagine that for ourselves. When the eight o'clock news came on, where you are watching live footage of bombings or piles of rubble, you can't imagine what it's like to live there. I have been thinking over the past few days that there must be some defence mechanism that protects us from looking straight into horrors. Conversely, none of us can imagine what it's like to be in Auschwitz, or to be Anne Frank. We can read, we can reflect, but there is something there that stops us from actually knowing what it is like to live in that way.

My second point might feel even more controversial. None of you can actually understand or feel what it's like to be an Israeli right now. I will suggest some paths perhaps towards that. If you were on a kibbutz when you were seventeen or have Israeli friends or have had a conversation with an Israeli, or you've read some literature you might feel you have an in. But, with all honesty, what we're stuck within is something we don't recognise either, so you definitely can't.

I have been thinking of this and the only time in my lifetime I can recall feeling similarly is not during a war. Not the first or second Gulf War, not the second Lebanon war, not countless rounds of violence on Gaza and not even the Intifada. The closest I have felt to what I am feeling right now is the day the COVID lockdown was announced when I was in the UK. Bear with me and I will explain.

Imagine a day in which everything you believed in is shattered to pieces. Imagine not being able to plan for the immediate or medium-term future. Imagine the anxiety that comes from this uncertainty, together with worry for your loved ones, and, well, for yourself.

Israelis woke up on the 7th October to a reality we never knew before. Our state had failed us completely. We were kidnapped from our homes and killed across our front yards. Our political differences were erased as we were left, completely vulnerable, with no response. Then the violence kept on coming, with manifold sirens, rockets demolishing homes. This is of course not a perfect comparison, but if you remember the first person you knew who died of COVID and how you felt then, amplify this 1200 times and this is where we are, collectively.

The moment I heard about 7th October I worried about the implications for the women and men of Gaza and the price they'll pay. But, we Israelis are all also processing our own grief.

A friend said to me that she can't bear to *watch* the news, she can't even imagine what it's like *living* the news. I think that's one of the most honest things said to me over the past fortnight and a huge step toward some kind of empathetic response at this moment. I think that we need to acknowledge boundaries of empathy and work from them. In the case of Gaza this is clear to most; but I want to say that this is also necessary in the case of Israel. I don't think empathy is essential in seeking justice: there are some common facts of humanity that lead us to know right from wrong. Killing babies is wrong; targeting civilians is wrong. We all should be safe in our homes. Let's start from there.

22.10.2023

## Making present that which is absent

My previous job focused on advocacy to ensure freedom of movement to and from Gaza. It remains to be seen what the organisation I worked for does "in the day after". It's clear the reality in which we'll live will not be the one we live in now nor the one before this attack, but it was an interesting experience and I learnt a lot about Gaza (mostly, that I don't know enough, after a year of international briefings and writing reports) as well as that Gaza is key for the entire region. The reason I wanted this focus is that the previous job at Peace Now refused to talk about Gaza; as they focused their efforts on the two-state solution (in the very classic 1990s constellation). Since Israel withdrew its ground forces and evicted settlements from Gaza in 2005 in the disengagement it is seen by some as no longer occupied, though Israel still controls all access to Gaza via land crossings and sea apart from one border in Egypt, hence the focus on freedom of movement, and the fact Gaza is still occupied de facto.

I recalled a few days ago that in the job interview I said that I wanted to work on Gaza as under a seventeen-year-old siege many governments (mine, but also others) have made it absent from my life and I should like to understand better how to make this land and its people present.

At Peace Now, I'd often hop in a car and go to the West Bank or East Jerusalem. There are severe restrictions on freedom of movement in the West Bank too and East Jerusalem has its own complexities, but there is no physical border in the city. There are atrocious things occurring all over Palestine. During the attacks on Gaza there has been a worrying rise in settler violence in the West Bank, which is also a façade to intensify the land grabs there. But Israelis can go and see for themselves what is happening there.

The Gaza Strip, however, is under siege. Israelis are not allowed in since the disengagement. Some people in the government have been talking of re-occupying Gaza and building new settlements there, a horrendous scenario. The average Israeli of my age has never been and can't go to Gaza. Israeli media hardly shows reality on the ground there (this round there have been critiques of that even from within Israel).

So, for circa a year I tried to understand, even if I realised it was impossible to feel, what this huge part of land that has been intentionally made absent for me is like.

I thought about this when I considered the Israelis taken hostage to Gaza. At this point, the Israeli army is estimating 210 women and men, babies and elderly citizens, have been abducted to Gaza. We do not know their state, whether they're alive, or in any state in which they can continue their lives. Two American citizens were released on Friday. But we do not know the fate of the rest.

I've been watching endless interviews with the abducted family members and talking to some of them. I know several people who've been abducted and/or their families. They sit in TV studios with eyes red from crying, holding a photograph, or a loved object, especially the parents of the children and babies holding soft toys their children loved is a consistent and heart-breaking sight. They tell stories about their loved ones. What they last remember of them. Their loved ones' plans for after that horrendous, dark Shabbat. They try to make present for us both their absent loved ones and what it is like to live without them, the absence itself...

I've tried to imagine what it is like to have someone I know snatched from me in one moment and in uncertain fate. The feeling was too horrendous to imagine. Many of the parents of the dead (over 1200) now say "we are the lucky ones, we are the ones who know". Imagine you do not know whether your grandchild or your grandmother is alive, or well, or sane. Imagine you do not know if she is tortured. Imagine the pain of that.

There are places our imaginations, including collective imaginations, get stuck at borders. I got stuck in a border trying to make Gaza present for myself in understanding this strip of land I live in. My government is stuck in making present its citizens and making them the first priority—saving them and bringing them back to their families.

Among the moral debate around Israel's bombardment of Gaza: is it proportional, is it conducted according to international law (reader: it's not) crept another conversation which is detached from law and morality and appeals to common sense. Families of the abducted have been repeatedly saying that as Israel does not know where the hostages are held, indiscriminate bombing, for one, endangers their loved ones. With every photo of a building brought to rubble they imagine their loved ones buried together with hundreds of Gazans under that rubble.

Perhaps we are able to imagine a different fate for ourselves, Israelis and Palestinians between the river and the sea, not only a shared fear of being buried under rubble but rather to somehow rebuild our shared spaces, if not together (considering the grave lack of trust this is further along the line), but at least with the recognition that if we are fated to die together we are fated to live together, and we will have to understand a way to make present all these absences which have been cruelly inserted into our lives.

It is clear the first moral imperative is to bring back the hostages safely to their families. Then we can begin to understand how to turn away from violence and towards grieving, rebuilding and finding a new way to live.

There must be something new under the Mediterranean sun.

24.10.2023

## The earth knows no war

Everyone around me, including myself, is moving through the past two weeks and looking ahead to the future in ebbs and flows. Some days are more tolerable than others. Some days we feel stronger and able to support others. Other days we can just about get dressed and get out of bed. Doom scrolling is hard to disengage from. Some days I have more faith in humanity. Other days I am fighting for hope. I am grateful for my community that is strong enough for us to support each other, but some days are really hard.

Today is such a day.

My comrade from the days in which I was Director of Peace

Now, Yotam Kipnis, had gone through two weeks thinking his parents were abducted. He learnt last week his father was killed. Last night he heard his mother died too in the massacre in Kibbutz Be'eri. He is an orphan. He is sitting shiva, mourning, for two weeks in a row over both his parents. I can't fathom the intensity of such grief.

I started my blog when my father died, during COVID. I remember feeling completely at loss, struggling to prepare food for myself or get dressed and organised. I was completely alone in the COVID lockdown. Yotam has a strong community of peace activists looking after him but I spent the morning feeling very sore-hearted and heavy for him. I'll go to the shiva tomorrow.

Yesterday I went to visit my cousin from a kibbutz down south which was under terrorist attack and by a combination of bravery and (honestly, I reckon) a miracle was spared. Her parents, brother and niece have been internally displaced.

She told me her brother was going back to the kibbutz, which has been suffering many rocket and missile bombardments daily, as it is time to sow the potatoes. I felt very emotional for that.

My family's kibbutz specialises in growing potatoes and peanuts among other things. I have strong childhood memories of my cousins coming to visit with huge bags of potatoes and peanuts, and then me and my mother preparing food out of them (there was a lot of potato-related cooking as well as home-roasted peanuts which were served over months on end). It is such a strong memory for me, those dirty bags, standing in our shelter, full of beautiful produce.

My family is scared, to say the least, that my cousin is going back to the kibbutz. But if you had any experience of working on the land you know that one cannot miss a time to sow, or a time to reap.

Before I went on my jolly jaunt to the USA and UK I was in touch with Palestinian farmers in the West Bank, with whom I've been working over the past few years in organising solidarity actions during olive harvest season. There has been a sharp escalation in settler violence against Palestinians in the West Bank. During harvest season settlers often come and try to interrupt the harvest, either by vandalising olive trees or even attacking the farmers directly as they harvest. When Israelis come to harvest often these attacks drop, as the settlers don't want to attack Jews, so literally just being there provides some kind of wall of security. Otherwise the farmers are afraid to access their olive groves.

I began organising these trips to the olive harvest before the war broke out. Then my contacts said it's too dangerous. You can't come over. It should be noted that settlers do attack those of us who come to harvest, as a lefty Jew is both a lefty and a Jew, and the settlers despise leftists *almost* as much as they despise Palestinians.

If you wonder where the Israeli army is in all of this, it often either overlooks the acts of violence towards Palestinians, joins them actively, or blocks Israeli leftists from coming near the groves. I have often found myself traipsing in the hills of the West Bank trying to avoid my own army blocking me from joining Palestinian farmers during harvest time.

Meanwhile, I've been thinking of the olive trees. Looking at the scarce trees I see in Tel Aviv, for beauty, not for use. I notice they are filling up with fruit, their branches getting heavy by the day.

The effects of these acts of violence against Palestinian farmers. is not only to deter them, this is violence against their livelihood, exasperating already harsh economic conditions. What will become of the olive groves?

A few days ago I got an email from my contact cautiously notifying us that the olive harvest together will commence shortly. I hope I can join soon.

I am thinking of my cousin going to sow the potatoes, and of the Palestinian farmers looking forward to harvesting olives. If there is something that gives me hope for this place is the ability to think about solidarity not as a vague, theoretical discussion, not as a conceptual relation, but enacted together in relation to the land.

The earth knows no war. Olives need to be harvested and potatoes need to be sown. We had our first rain the other day; usually a joyous day in this land affluent with deserts. The days are getting shorter. It is cool enough to wear a cardigan in the evening. There is a gentle breeze that sweeps my face when I come home in the evenings. David, our friendly building cat, is growing his winter fur.

Perhaps if people were able to think of each other and the land with more gentleness, away from violence, with care and consideration, we'd see an end to war.

My cousin who is returning to his kibbutz has lost several friends and comrades in this attack. I think of his resilience and hope, for the days it will be time to reap the potatoes. And care for olive trees after the harvest.

And same again.

## My world is broken

I didn't sleep at all last night. We in Tel Aviv can hear the bombardment of Gaza. It's only 100km away. We had several alarms, which now feel like an exhausting routine. Israeli sources hardly report the violent attack on Gaza. I follow some sources though I doubt there can be *any* truly objective reporting of anything, let alone a crisis of this scale, but that's for a different discussion.

Throughout the last few days, as we became accustomed to this routine which is truly beyond comprehension, I've felt a deepening sense of grief. It is not only the death and absence all around us, talking to friends and family who are waiting for their loved ones to return or attending various events commemorating the sudden, abrupt loss of life. It is a loss of a world we lived in three weeks ago.

There have been various, bloody, horrific incursions that Israel has taken on Gaza. Their price on Palestinian life was heavy. This incursion is not only deviant in its magnitude, around 7000 people have died and out of them 3000 children. But its context and the way it unfolded is different.

There were several things that for me were not surprising and did not break my world. The atrocities that Hamas committed were horrifying yet not surprising. The oppressive regime that Hamas is sustaining in Gaza against its own people has taught me enough about their cruelty and the fact that they are not 'freedom fighters'. However, the loss of feeling of safety in my own home, despite not being new—we all lived through several wars, terrorist attacks and operations—yet the way these attacks unfolded has swept the earth from under our feet.

Israel's lack of compliance with international law is not surprising to me either. If you know me outside of reading these essays, and/or had read any of my books and/or followed my career, you know that the attempt to hold Israel accountable has become a lifelong mission for me and a red thread throughout everything I do. However, once again, the way that these attacks against Gazans is unfolding, while, it should be stressed, endangering the lives of Israeli hostages being kept there, has been a startling awakening call. Those people abducted could have been me, and my government would have done nothing to return me while carrying out vicious vendettas and crimes against humanity.

While all these events you're all following are unfolding, the Israeli government is furthering a vicious crackdown on freedom of speech, especially against Palestinian citizens of Israel, but against anyone who dares raise their voice against the war. Even a call for a ceasefire is considered unpatriotic. Some people were fired from their jobs just for dissenting from the government. We all know our communications are under surveillance. People have been arrested for Facebook posts over the past week. So, once again, when you write to your Israeli friends and ask 'why don't you dissent' please remember we live in a climate of fear, where everything we say is under a chilling effect, and many of us worry for our families and relatives who might be impacted as a result of our actions.

The Israeli police had passed a decision, since reversed, forbidding protesting on political grounds during the war. I wonder what one can protest during a war that is not on political grounds? I am proud to say that nevertheless there has been a protest organised this evening, which I will attend, calling to prioritise bringing back hostages and for a ceasefire. This was due to take place even against police regulations. But, once again, the price we are paying for this action takes manifold prisms.

Over the past week I have felt myself sink more and more into indescribable fatigue. It's not just the nocturnal alarms and lack of sleep, but rather the feeling of loss of a grasp on reality, and consequently the struggle to sustain hope. It is clear to us all that what had been before the 7th October won't return, that we need to rebuild from scratch. But in order to rebuild one needs a connection to the world, to sense it, to feel it. Right now the horrors are just too vast. I am living in the midst of a genocide carried in my name, and a witch hunt against anyone daring to name it as such. Keeping to the narrative that has led me all my life, believing that human rights and humanity are the way out of darkness into the light has become a struggle in its own right. Keeping to that thought is now the thing I am fighting with the most. Yesterday I went to a collective reading of Eliot's *The Waste Land*. I recall here a different quotation of his: "humankind cannot bear very much reality". I feel that at this moment I am fighting to both bear the reality I need to bear, and to be able to fight on for justice, out of that moment of recognition and reckoning.

My world is broken. I need to pick up the pieces of what I had believed in, what I had loved, what I had fought for, and create a new narrative to make sense of the world. Some of it will continue from before the 7th October but much of it will be new. And in this process of building the world anew, understanding how we can still fight for justice, for empathy, for solidarity, I will need to keep tender and open, strong and fierce, humble and confident, disciplined and compassionate. This is true for all of us Israelis who believe this land can and has to do better.

29.10.2023

## Discussed: Love comes more naturally to the human heart than its opposite

While the entire world is watching and discussing Gaza, I am thinking of another aspect of events unravelled on the 7th October.

Over the past few years, and certainly under this government, the most radical and overtly Jewish supremacist in the history of the country, relationships between Palestinians and Israelis have become more volatile and heightened. Both within the context of occupation (West Bank, Gaza, East Jerusalem) but also inside Israel, where about 20% of the population are Palestinian citizens of Israel. Some of these Palestinians relate to the political issues around the occupation, but some of them do not. Some of them refer to themselves as 'Arabs', some of them accentuate their Palestinian identity.

I think one huge element that is missed in the pro-Israel/pro-Palestinian discussion abroad is just how intertwined our lives are here. Across the border, certainly, but especially within Israel.

About six months ago I had a breast cancer scare. I come from a family with a sadly rich history of cancer, and after repressing what I clearly felt was a lump, I finally scheduled an appointment to see my doctor who sent me for urgent tests. I didn't discuss this widely as I had a very rocky relationship with my then boss, and had felt insecure in so many ways around her and others. Luckily, the tests were done swiftly and came back benign, though the doctors did see some things that worried them and ordered me to have a six months check up. These six months occurred this week.

No appointments were available around where I am, so I scheduled one in Jerusalem. This is a city in which so many of us are stuck side by side: secular Jews, religious Jews, Palestinian citizens of Israel, Palestinians who live in East Jerusalem, without a clear border and all somehow forced to live together. I arrived doubly nervous; obviously the situation was stressful as it is, but doing all this during a war (will there be an alarm when I'm en route? will there be one when I'm being checked?) added to my anxiety which I guess was apparent.

Throughout the entire process the woman who examined me was Palestinian. She treated me with outstanding kindness, recognising my vulnerability and caring for it. It was clear that she was tired—we all are, these days—and I was tired and anxious. She could tell I was anxious and went above and beyond to calm me down. As I was buttoning up my shirt I thought about the fact that beyond all political debates, we are all destined to live together and, when the sticks are down, compassion is a very natural sentiment.

On Thursday I attended a meeting regarding organising for this time. There has been incitement from the government, and especially one Minister, Itamar Ben Gvir (an overtly Kahanist who has been convicted of Jewish terrorism) who, with his collaborators, is trying to create tensions between Palestinians and Israelis within the Green Line. In the face of that, in mixed cities mixed guards have been established to defend and protect each other. In Yaffa 500 people attended a Zoom that was organised to establish that guard including Palestinians and Jewish Israelis, and many others around the country were formed too. There are collective efforts—Jewish and Palestinian—to assist those impacted by the Hamas attack in the unrecognised Bedouin villages which displaced many who already were impoverished and oppressed before the attacks. I cannot stress enough how brave and important these initiatives are at this moment in time. Not only do they swim strongly against the stream of racism and violence, but they create an infrastructure of a different future; of those motivated by compassion and love and care for the other rather than hatred and violence.

I feel strongly that the future of this strip of land—whatever political solution may come about here, and honestly now I am partial to the solution that would allow us all to live somehow together—depends on moving to this collaboration based on care. Looking at Jewish history, and at international responses to the 7th October, I can understand the dread arising in many of my friends that pushes them to hatred, despair, angst and fear of those around them. Of course, for Palestinians the fear and disbelief of

43

their fellow countrymen and women is also very easy to understand considering an overtly genocidal unfolding of events.

I want to say here that the toughest and most urgent thing we can do is to transcend those urges. I am not a wishy washy liberal calling for peace and love. I think the hardest thing to find after your people have been massacred is the ability to see those who didn't kill you still as people with whom you need to live, and that this would be much easier if you didn't hate them.

I cannot stress enough how important the structures are that enable us, Israelis and Palestinians from all sides of the border, to know each other, to recognise the human in each other and to subvert the politics that are claimed are ours. We need to acknowledge wrongs, yes, but we also need to look into the future and realise that we are all stuck here and destined to live together so we need to do so as humans and not as pawns in political football.


One running theme of these notes has been to shift away from the politics of revenge and towards the politics of human rights, international law and accountability. After hearing of a lynching attempt of Palestinian citizens of Israel in a college I couldn't repress the first thought that came to my mind this morning. I wish the entire American aid monies would be used for education. It could be used for us all, between the river and the sea, to know each other as people. To have tough conversations, yes, but also to look into our future together and think how we want to mould it. I wish Biden would tell Netanyahu that due to his lack of compliance with international law from now on all American aid goes to co-existence education. Not empty dialogue meetings that avoid difficult questions. Not intellectual debates leading to gotcha arguments, who has the strongest slogans, who gets more famous to align with us. People, normal, ordinary people, who want to live their lives, sitting together and understanding where they went wrong and what they can do to right that. Finding a course for reparations but also to work together, truly, against the hatred and incitement instilled in us from day one of our lives.

Nelson Mandela was a consistent comrade to the Palestinian struggle, and his legacy has been whitewashed, something I am critical of and want to turn away from. However this quote of his resonates in my mind, as I oppose my genocidal government and fight hard to keep the hope for a better future for all between the river and the sea.

> "No one is born hating another person because of the colour of his skin, or his background, or his religion. People must learn to hate, and if they can learn to hate, they can be taught to love, for love comes more naturally to the human heart than its opposite."
>
> (from Long Walk to Freedom)

# NOVEMBER

There is no path to peace,
peace is the path

## All grief is equal

Yesterday was a strange and sad day. I heard of two people in my orbit who were killed. A few months ago the organisation in which I worked hosted an open meeting about Gaza. On Zoom, a gentle and deep thinker, a teacher from Gaza, Khalil, was speaking. He gave an eloquent analysis of his own condition— besieged for seventeen years—and spoke of his hope that education would transform the lives of his family and especially his students. I spoke to a colleague who connected us and we were in touch with him after that, he was keen to keep the conversation going. Yesterday he, and his entire family, were killed by the Israeli army.

Yesterday a good friend's cousin, a soldier in the Israeli army, was killed. All accounts of him were of a gentle soul who was called for service but just wanted to live his life. His Instagram account shows beautiful photographs capturing tranquil scenes, even when already in Gaza. His last photograph, taken on the morning of his death, was of a dog and an empty guard tower.

And so, I was pondering the odd position of grieving for both sides. When these instances occur, and when I discuss them with people outside of Israel, they often get interpreted as equivocation. As if all losses are equal and glossing over power inequalities. But you see, all grief is equal.

The question of dead soldiers is one that had weighed heavily on me when I lived in the UK. I could never openly say I was sad when a soldier died. The anxiety of waiting to hear the names announced, or social media announcing—please god may it not be someone I know, but it's always someone one knows. Israel has conscription duty, and in this round 300,000 people were called into reserve duty. Most of my male friends, including some incredible lefty activists, had gone. When the question of refusal is raised I can say, briefly, that like many cases of civil disobedience it is not an automatic reaction to peace-loving sentiment. In Israel, many basic rights depend on conscription or being released for religious reasons, so it takes an amount of support and privilege to be able to do so.

And here I am apologising to you for grieving with my friend for his cousin.

Equally, I had found some approaches considering Palestinian grief one-sided and flat though it's less for me to critique them. The Palestinians who recognise us Israeli lefties as allies, even imperfect ones, and connect with us despite everything are often seen as lesser heroes of resistance. Those who understand the complexity of where we are at and that one can be an oppressor and yet hope and work for better days do not always get the space they deserve. Hatred, on both sides, is much more popular.

Yesterday, after I got the news, I tweeted about this sensation of dual grief. It took less than a day for someone to tweet at me "did your friend kill children". It feels that there is a lot of darkness around us right now.

I am Israeli. I served in the military. I worked in the education field, as by that point I had known the reality of life on the West Bank in the 1990s and did not want part of that. Many of my kind-hearted, hopeful friends are right now in the depth of a war they did not choose to fight. Many had left families and friends impacted by the 7th October massacres. My friends are not fuelled by genocidal hatred nor do they wish to kill Palestinian children. They want their families to be safe and their kids to have a better future than their own.

I felt very heavy for Khalil and his family. Quite honestly, I can totally understand the anger and hatred that Israeli occupation generates. All the more reason I think it's so rare and admirable for those to think further and deeper, to reflect on how education can transform lives and how working with your allies—who are positioned to you as your enemies—can make a difference in the world.

Grief is heavy. Grief is hard. A mother who loses her child is torn forever. A family wiped off the face of the earth like it never existed is unimaginable.

Gentle souls that are no more.

04.11.2023

## 4.11.1995, 7.10.2023, 10,000.
## Fighting for hope and humanity

Today marks twenty-eight years since the assassination of Yizkhak Rabin, the last Israeli leader who worked in any kind of seriousness towards a political resolution and an end to the occupation. Today also marks four weeks since the 7th October attacks. In Jewish faith, thirty days mark the end of the mourning period, but in a way, after we had understood what had occurred here we are only now beginning to grieve properly.

We are nearly at the horrific marker of 10,000 dead in Gaza due to Israeli attacks.

I feel over the past few weeks my own biggest battle has been to fight for hope that things can be different than the current reality, Israel keeping Gaza under its thumb and going into rounds of violence, some worse than others. Israelis living in fear, and if they engage the Palestinian cause, shame. Feeling always that something horrific is around the corner, and after 7th October being validated that this indeed is true. Being afraid of turning on the news. Feeling ashamed at what my government is doing. Also feeling anxious for myself, family and friends, alone in that anxiety, and mainly not knowing what the best way out of this loop of hopelessness is.

The recent weeks have also taken a substantial toll on our humanity. Responses both to the 7th October attacks as well as Israeli attacks on Gaza had made us all, both here between the river and the sea, and around the world, suspicious, anxious, polarised. The need to take human suffering and put it into soundbites that would fit into Instagram stories makes the complexity of humanity disappear. Many of us Israelis are far from condoning the actions of our government in Gaza. We also want to live safely and don't know the best way forward to achieve that. Our friends are fighting in the Strip. We are struggling to understand the horrors of death and destruction in Gaza. An Israeli friend said to me: I am trying to feel empathy but the devastation is so huge; how can one feel empathetic to 10,000 dead people?

The assassination of Rabin was my own political turning point. I was thirteen. I was shocked and horrified and felt a void, not unlike the one I'm feeling now. I had gone to school and attended all the ceremonies and commemorations and we had special classes discussing the horridness of this political murder. A friend from school told me she was going to meetings of Peace Now. I decided to go along. I went over the border and saw colonisation in my eyes. I saw the settlements and saw Palestinians whose land was stolen. I understood what it would mean for me to dissent against my own people. Back then, the Israeli left was in government and there were many more of us than now. But still, the feeling of constantly speaking up against our leadership is one that remains with me.

It's very popular now to put down the Oslo Accords, show the partiality of their vision and the fact they were unsustainable from the get-go. The truth is, politically, we lack a counterfactual. Netanyahu was elected for the first time soon after the murder of Rabin and most of my adult life has been in the shadow of his premiership, spurring hatred and division. Rabin may have got many things wrong (again, we don't know), but there is one thing he had given my generation: a sense of hope. The feeling that things can be different. I remember watching with my family Rabin shake hands with Yasser Arafat, whom I only knew from Israeli media as a 'terrorist'. I remember a specific speech, one I only appreciated properly later on, in which Rabin gave his Army number and then stated peace was the only option. In the end, those of us who want to see a different Israel will need people like Rabin, who've been in the depth of the war machine, have said some offensive statements regarding Palestinians and the occupation, and then started to turn. A lot of ink has been spilled about the danger of Generation Z doing their politics on

Instagram and Twitter, so I won't add to that; but perhaps the biggest danger of reducing our political life to that kind of politics is that there is no room for error. If you post something in full passion and then a day, week, month, ten years later feel you've made a mistake, you can delete the post perhaps but your voice is there, with all the responses it spurred at the time. There is no place to say: I was wrong, I have changed. Or simply: I don't know.

I feel that in fighting for humanity: the ability to stop the killing in Gaza but also grieve and understand the trauma in Israel we need to be able to say: I don't know.

What I do know is that we need to save space for those of us who are willing to change, to admit we were wrong. Those who don't want to moralise or take revenge but who wish for a better life for all living between the river and the sea. Who want to feel, very terribly badly, the sensation of hope running through their veins. Who don't want to win the argument, but to be proven wrong when things are better than they expected.

Yesterday I hosted a reading group in which we read the poetry of a Gazan poet, Basem Al-Nabriss, who had been exiled from the Strip after Hamas took power there, in correspondence with the Israeli poet and woman of letters Tal Nitzan. Even just publishing the event brought some harassment upon the bookstore that hosted the event. In the end, it was a tender meeting; we read and discussed our fears, the fact that we still don't know what had happened to us on the 7th October but that words and poetry matter, listening to human beings that geopolitical borders make us deaf towards. It was a meeting of shared humanity, of grieving and of hoping that we can extend this shared humanity beyond where we are. I wish some of the air we breathed there, when we sat under the trees and read about the beauty of Gaza through Al-Nabriss's eyes, could spread beyond, that we can kindle this little moment of hope and humanity and spread it further, like wind. That we would all feel safe in our homes.

05.11.2023

## Dancing through grief

I started this blog during COVID, a time of collective grief though different from the one I'm experiencing now. This was also a time of grief for me personally. My father passed away on Monday 30th March 2020. I was still living in Oxford and was on the phone with my mother in Israel when she got the news. I remember not understanding but realising that my world has shifted. That afternoon I had planned to take an online dance class. The UK was not under lockdown yet but the US and parts of Europe were. I decided, with advice from friends, to still take the class (dance friends: it was a Graham class with Lloyd Knight, which as you know is the essence of beauty and grace personified).

Over the next few months I had taken dance classes online while grieving for my father and understanding the new world around me. Collective grief became entangled with my own personal grief, and the very acute sensation of being separated from my mother as we were mourning on two sides of the world. I can't say I was feeling lonely because I didn't understand what I was feeling. In hindsight I understood that in addition to being shaken by losing my father—losing a parent is a shock no matter when that happens—I was shaken by losing a world I knew and understood. That time was punctured with moments of intense immersion. I applied myself to reading. Specifically, I started with Proust's *In Search of Lost Time*, which my father had read in its entirety and I had always wanted to read, and writing. I finished writing two books, my *Rosa Luxemburg* and *Dance & Activism* during the lockdown, in parallel. I also experimented with dance. I had taken online classes with renowned Cunningham dancer Andrea Weber—whom I am proud to now call a friend but has been an ongoing inspiration—and learnt Cunningham technique for the first time in my life. The diligence and scrutiny of each movement, as we took twice weekly Zoom classes gave me more breath and energy than I can put in words. The angle of our backs mattered. How we held our breath or not mattered. Immersing ourselves in the movement mattered. When things that had mattered so much to me were taken away from me abruptly having this constant, this dedication to beauty and grace were a ritual and a lifeline. I don't think I could have got through these months without these Zooms.

A year later I came back to Israel to work in politics. Now, three years after that period, I find myself dancing through grief again.

Yesterday I went to a large rally advocating the release of the hostages from Gaza. There were tens of thousands of people there, impressive especially in a time of a war, when there could have been an alarm at any moment. There was indeed one an hour after we got home. I ran into many people I knew from human rights/left circles, but then I stumbled into a circle of dance people I knew. We all hugged tiredly and sighed. Then we started talking about getting back into work (there were mostly choreographers but one other dance writer). Many spoke of how hard it had been to get back into the studio. One choreographer I especially love and admire, Yasmeen Godder, spoke about a feeling of physical sickness the moment she stepped back into the studio. But she felt the dancers and students needed that and that in turn nourished her. Dance is not only physical practice, it is also a community. It's a place where you don't talk but move together. When everything is so polarised being in a space in which no talking is pretty much the most fundamental rule obeyed, that is so precious and so necessary.

Not that politics can be left outside of the studio, of course. One of my ballet teachers had bombarded me with pro-Israel Hasbara videos, pushing the Government's official narrative, to the extent I felt I had to block her on social media and forgo her classes. Luckily, my favourite teacher, Gabrielle Neuhaus, is brilliant both as a conversation partner and as a ballet teacher.

Classes here started about a week after 7th October and the war broke out. Dancers are without work as performances are banned due to public safety measures; no large gatherings of people indoors are allowed. There was a hunger for places where people could come together in a safe way but also to give some kind of routine. Things are nowhere near normal. It is apparent people are afraid to speak and make small talk, as you don't know who had been implicated in death and war, and how. So far I've only had one alarm during class but it's an ever looming danger and possibility. So you're always in heightened expectation to have to run back into "the real world".

This kind of grief is different to COVID's collective grief and for me, the grief I went through while losing my father. It is collective, and political, and politicised. It feels everyone has an opinion on who should grieve and how. And so, moving and not speaking feels like a generative practice.

It is hard to explain dancing at times like this. There is no real joy though the body responds to movement and gives punctured moments of pleasure. For an hour and a half you care about where your legs go and how to keep the best focus on multiple turns. For an hour and a half you focus on practice and on looking deep into yourself. Of course, the outside world is never far. I find myself fighting thoughts during class and then just letting go when these thoughts come, just immersing myself in them while moving. And so I find myself dancing with and through fear, and anxiety, and immense sadness, and anger, and also moments of uplift and then more often than not, guilt for feeling these moments of uplift. For an hour and a half my mind is constantly pulled towards my body. For an hour and a half I am a student and try to improve within myself, and don't have to speak about anything or defend anything or combat anything. I am just this week's me, trying to do better than last week's me.

In my third book I wrote about ballet in Gaza. It is unsurprising that ballet has been a source of resilience and empowerment for so many, including those I am taught to know as my enemies. There are moments I experience intense guilt when thinking about dance. Why am I entitled to dance and they aren't? And then I tell myself that my deepest faith and belief is that dance is, for those of us for whom it is an inextricable part of our life, a way to be human. And so I wish and pray that when Gaza is rebuilt ballet schools will not be pushed to the end of the priority list, though I know well there are urgent things to tend to.

These days I mix my weeks with two ballet classes and two Gaga classes. I take one ballet class (today's) en pointe. One of my joyful revelations has been finding a ballet teacher I adore. Gabrielle Neuhaus is a wonderful performance artist, razor sharp, an excellent feminist (which matters as we get to do a lot of "boys' exercises"; ballet is very gendered). She is also open and generous and lovely to chat with, which means classes are an important community for me to feed off. I am grateful to have found Gabrielle and returned to ballet, a year ago this December.

I hadn't done pointe work in five years and this is my challenge and my deep meditation within my embodied self. The pain and the pleasure of seeking to find more balance, literally and figuratively, enables me to focus in a very deep way.

Gaga is a movement language invented by Ohad Naharin, house choreographer of the Batsheva dance company, Israel's paramount dance company. It is unlike anything I ever did before. Gaga works through imagery and instructions that channel your movement, which is an hour of free improvisation, meaning not copying the teacher but doing your own thing. The images can shift from "imagine you are moving through honey" to "imagine you are like spaghetti in boiling water". I feel deeply that Gaga is everything that is beautiful and also difficult in Israel. It is an explosion of energy and lack of order. It is very Israeli. Because Ohad gives daily classes to the teachers and dancers, Tel Aviv is the mecca for Gaga people, and it feels very grounded here, even more now as many of the international members of the dance community, as well as generally internationals in Tel Aviv, had fled since the war broke out. So it has become even more local.

I am a person with a very short attention span and so having to listen to constant instructions is excellent for me. It keeps me thinking away from the last disturbing piece of analysis I read or what is the next thing I have to do and how futile it feels. There is a bit of a cult around Gaga which means we regulars know each other, and there is a feeling of community heightened by the abnormal situation we dance in. I think it says a lot about the resilience of the dance community here that these classes are not only ongoing but expanding.

When I dance these days I find a mix of heaviness and light, sadness and moments of joy then flipping back into reality outside of the studio. I find discipline and strength and vulnerability and horror. And love. A lot of love. For movement in itself and for people who dedicate themselves to movement. For that moment in which I am reminded to bring down my shoulders in order to turn better, as if it's the most important thing in the world. For a moment, it is. And I hold on to that moment for the days, weeks, months to come.

Thanks again for reading and talking to me from wherever you are. One day we'll all be able to dance and not grieve. For now, we continue to move forward, and pray and work for a better tomorrow.


06.11.2023


One month ago today

Tomorrow will mark a month since the Hamas attacks, but I wanted to mark a month before our lives shifted, and take stock of what has changed, what has not changed and what is in flux and will be for a while.

One month ago today I boarded a night flight from NYC to London. I had a magical and rejuvenating time in NYC. Many of the people who made it so are reading this essay, so thank you. After some ups and downs personally and professionally (which feel like nothing today, part of the transformation I'm going through) I felt like myself again. I had talked about my books and I had danced and I met friends and walked the streets of NYC.

When the flight landed and I switched on my phone I got two cryptic and short messages. One from a next door neighbour who asked me if I was still abroad. I didn't know why she had asked but I replied "yes" and she said "good". Then I got a confusing text from Tel Aviv municipality, two hours previously, stating that due to the new emergency everyone would have to evacuate to the bomb shelter. I was puzzled but started to understand what was happening.

The days passed and I realised I had both known and did not know what was happening. I both understood and did not understand. This is an ever present feeling that is with me since then and till now, and will accompany me—us—for a while. I can now take stock of what has or has not changed.

I oppose, morally and politically, indiscriminate targeting of civilians. When it comes to defending Palestinian human rights I have been saying this for all of my adult life. When it comes to defending Israeli life, I have felt vividly, this is a new sensation. A war crime of heinous magnitude had been committed against my family and friends. And I had to process what it was like, for once, not only critiquing my government for violence used in my name for decades, but also violence enacted on my people. Of course, Israeli civilians had been targeted in terrorism attacks and other hate crimes, but something like this hadn't occurred in my adult life.

My politics hasn't changed. My morality hasn't changed. I still oppose injustice enacted in my name, abusing human rights, and violating people's personhood under ideological guises. I deplore that when it is done in my name and when it is done to my people. I am also by nature a pragmatic and rational person who wants to shift towards solutions that ensure maximum safety for all in a just way, while acknowledging that no solution is perfect and sustainability and future looking solutions are better than those who enact revenge under the guise of justice.

My alliances have shifted. My relationships have shifted. I have been going back to the late, great Tony Judt who had quoted John Maynard Keynes: "when the facts change, I change my mind". In the question of Israel and Palestine the facts change all the time, including the narratives that are given to the history of both peoples. It is not only that the situation in Israel/Palestine has changed, the global narrative around it has shifted. For me, the questions that had been bothering me since I started to engage politics here when I was thirteen, so nearly thirty years ago, had been changing but also remained open-ended. I work very much in documenting current land grabs and colonisation in vivo. But something shifted in me over the last few weeks; when I saw people using concepts I had been using to justify violence against my people. If you are using three quotes from Fanon to justify having babies and old people snatched from their beds at 6am because of their identity, you are not my comrade. In the name of easy distinction between victim and wrongdoer, right from wrong, the good and the bad, some people had lost their humanity and basic common sense.

My first and only benchmark for the people with whom I choose to engage is humanity and empathy. That hasn't changed. This has been a month of intense grief. We are losing people every day, and our hearts are breaking again and again. This has been a month of being torn to our bone, of being unsafe in our homes.

One big change that had occurred to me over the past month, is understanding that there is a limit to how much people can understand me.

When I lived in the UK I realised after a while I cannot understand to the core of being British, or rather, being English, as I only ever lived in England. The things I admired while visiting as a tourist remained as distant to me as in my last day in England as resident. Equally, when I lived in the USA or engaged Americans, I felt very deeply that I cannot understand Americans. There is a way in which there is such a thing as Americanism that I will never understand.

What I'm coming to realise now, is that equally, many in the diaspora don't understand Israeliness. There is at times an attempt to usurp our voices, to co-opt them for various ideological positions, which we might agree with or not, but that remains an act of co-optation rather than actually listening to us. But something in our upbringing puts us in a different position to the way others engage the question of Israel/Palestine. I am really grateful to those who said to me "I can't imagine how you feel", as that has been the first step towards an honest dialogue.

I am both myself and not myself. Many of you who know me outside of these notes know I love to dance, and write and drink and read and immerse myself in joy and beauty in the world. That part of me has been on hold, in a void, for a month. I am thinking and writing and inquiring but, like everyone around me, my resilience has been chopped to the ground. I am tired of hearing from people when they need something of me, as for once, I need something from many people. I need to hold a space to be broken for a bit, to be me but also a less joyful, unequivocal and firm me. And so, a month ago I was a different person and all the changes of this month will mean I will probably not be the same person exactly again. But my intent to fight for what is right and what ensures safety for all, Jews and Palestinians, between the river and the sea remains intact. We all deserve both safety and joy.

07.11.2023

## Real war, fake news

Today is a month since 7th October passed. It both feels like an hour and a decade ago. Frankly, I'm still so emotionally confused about it all, I decided to write today about something that has been bothering me for a long time which is also invoked by reading Naomi Klein's new book I wrote about a few days ago.

I thought I'd start with some basics and then share some of my experience, relevant to the events of the past month.

Here's the thing. All involved share fake news/conflate facts/inflate facts/go on hyperboles/underestimate facts when it works for their narrative. No one who has a stake in this war—

and if you have an opinion you have a stake in the war—is sharing 'objective' reality. Reality is not objective, and everything can be read from multiple perspectives. Plus, and this is important to stress, those of us directly implicated, living through this war, cannot detach ourselves from our realities.

I thought it might be helpful to share some past experience, as someone who has worked in politics/human rights in Israel/Palestine. I discovered, very quickly, that fake news was everywhere. Videos can be fabricated, dates on photographs changed; old media items recycled and new twists applied to uncomfortable data, making it lose its meaning completely. My direct experience started with working in settlement expansion, a field in which *everyone* had stakes in changing the data and its framing. Israeli officials wanted to underestimate settlement growth. Palestinians wanted to show how vast it had been, and, ironically, the settlers themselves had the same incentive, to show how their project is thriving. So, when hearing of a new outpost or a new neighbourhood approved, or hearing of a home taken over in East Jerusalem, we always had to compare and contrast multiple sources. I want to say, to a large extent, I understand everyone's motivation in twisting the data, but this makes a really miserable life for those of us who just want to know *what happened*. I am not a post-modernist. I believe there are some things in the world that exist and we know them to be what they are. But in order to get to that moment of knowing, especially when working in this field, there are many, many twists and turns to be taken in order to challenge the many, many twists and turns taken by all parties.

I had once, when I was Director of Peace Now, fallen victim to fake news. The settlers released some news on further steps to firm up one of the illegal outposts in the West Bank and legalise it. I worked frantically opposite my media director. We wrote a tweet and a press release, and I was going to apply pressure to the members of Knesset who had been on our side of things to bring this to the forefront and not only stop it but stop these dangerous trends.

Reader: there were no such steps. There was no further push to legalise the outpost. The settler lobby released this info so that someone would fall for that bait and respond to it. They did. It was me.

We quickly retracted the Tweet and sent a correction but the damage had been done. Screenshots shaming us and showing how gullible and 'self-hating Jews' we had been to fall for that information and respond to it hyperbolically (which of course we did, to exert public pressure). I had learned my lesson. I never wrote *anything* without fact-checking with various sources. I am still worried about what I'm sharing and how.


When it comes to Gaza things are even more complex. Gaza has been under Israeli siege for seventeen years. It is one of the most densely populated regions between the river and the sea. Even in so-called 'peaceful' days (when one is under siege, when is it actually peaceful?) it is oftentimes hard to know exactly the unfolding of events, to verify who is involved, and how. Fact-checking takes much, much longer even not during an Israeli campaign on Gaza. I personally operate with a deep doubt for both 'official' narratives as neither is particularly independent. Organisations that operate in Gaza are subjected to the same bureaucratic violence Gazan citizens are subjected to. They rarely have a better bird's eye view of events. Even in peaceful times. Both Hamas and the Israeli authorities terrorise anyone operating in Gaza, and exercise censorship in multiple ways, directly and indirectly. Both authorities also have an interest in fixing data and media so it fits their narrative.

Since going into this line of work I've grown extra suspicious (not that a DPhil in political theory makes one trusting of sources!). I double-check what I share, and yet I am positive I probably shared unverified news and analysis. I am lucky and privileged to know sources and those with contacts on the ground, so I try to share news from them, but again, I'm sure we all fall for it.

Between the war on narrative and fake news there is one element that has really got to me, more than I'd like to admit. That is that strand of thinking that sees Hamas murders and kidnapping exactly a month ago as either fake (done by the Israeli Army) or fabricated completely. Although I find it upsetting also seeing those who justify the attacks I can deal more easily with them in my mind; at least we agree that this has *happened*, and the judgement on its consequences differ.

First, may I tell you, as someone who's worked (sadly for me) opposite Israeli military press releases, and has worked on Gaza and the West Bank, I can tell you if Israel wanted to bomb Gaza it didn't have to go into this elaborate exercise. Simply Google 'Israeli attacks on Gaza' over the past fifteen years and see how many there have been.

Secondly, and here is where it gets personal, I know for myself some of the people involved. Killed. Abducted. Grieving. I've been following testimonies, and this is not on some abstract media source. These are my friends and comrades, sharing their worst day in their life. This is my family sharing how it miraculously got saved.

There is a point in doing such documenting work at which one starts to gaslight oneself. Has this thing actually happened? Am I right in perceiving this? I often copy-pasted about five times and re-read and juxtaposed when especially heinous data came through to my desk. But, here's the thing. When my friends and family tell me their story first-hand I don't need to fact-check. And I can't allow myself to sink so low.

There is of course also an accusation of 'Pallywood', faking violence and death, often hurled by some Israelis. But the evidence from Gaza is horrific enough. There is ample coming through, fact-checked and verified.

As for the consequences, conclusions and what we can learn, the bigger picture, in my professional capacity here I'm forgoing judgement for a while. It feels like Instagram and Twitter have become tribunals, but in the fog of war I'd rather wait to get all the facts when we know they are facts, and not a post uploaded and retracted which had become 'evidence' in a field trial.

At the same time I can assure you all this war is very real. I'm living through it every day. I'll keep doubting the news but believing the victims and survivors, as it feels like the only thing left of humanity in the midst of this horrific moment.

## From the River to the Sea, on anti-Semitism (including on the left), and two asks if you're marching this weekend to defend human rights

I woke up to read that Rashida Tlaib, the Palestinian–American Member of Congress was censored for saying 'from the river to the sea' (and other things). Unlike many of my fellow Israelis, I'm not pleased about that. I don't think censorship, especially of a Palestinian leader in this context is justifiable, and I also think this might have terrible counter-results, as I'll explain below.

Over the past weeks, I've been going back to read Arendt's *The Origins of Totalitarianism* as well as Zigmunt Bauman's accounts of the Holocaust in the context of modernity. I've turned back to both, among other reasons, to think carefully of genocide and what leads to it, but en route found some very thought-provoking and helpful writing on anti-Semitism. I'm toying with the idea of writing something more formal myself on anti-Semitism going back to those texts, but for now I will share my personal experiences and thoughts. This is not only an intellectual exercise. I'll ask of you, something I hadn't done before, two concrete things if indeed you see yourself as defenders of human rights and especially if you're marching this weekend for Gaza. But later.

I'm going to write some things that might be unpopular with *everyone*, but I'm trying to work with distinctions, not least, as my own thinking is always inspired by Arendt.

As opposed to many of my countrymen, and certainly, the mainstream Israeli media, I do not think chanting 'from the river to the sea', in and of itself, is anti-Semitic. As I have written here in the past, all peaceful solutions that would bring lasting peace to this fraught region would have to recognise and respond to the Nakba, the mass killings and displacement that occurred before 1948 and gave way to the Jewish state. As I have also written here, many of the people living in Gaza are not "Gazans", but are refugees displaced from their villages and towns in and before 1948. So claiming freedom for them isn't in and of itself anti-Semitic.

I do think intent is very important here and sadly this is not something that one can decipher in a march. If you're chanting 'from the river to the sea' thinking any step forward from here will demand recognition, reparation and some kind of restorative and transitional justice acknowledging the Nakba, I'm with you.

But, I am not naive, and know very well there are some people who chant 'from the river to the sea' meaning make Israelis disappear from this bit of land, we don't care how. This is genocidal and anti-Semitic.

In the same way that is both helpful and problematic, I guess, I spent my adult life saying that critiquing the Israeli state isn't in and of itself anti-Semitic. I also think singling out the only Jewish state isn't in and of itself a sign of anti-Semitism. It's very clear to me, both as an Israeli but also as a political theorist, that Palestine/Israel is a liminal space, a boundary, if you will, in which many discourses are fought out. I understand why the settler colonial discourse internationally has taken hold here, though I still am not convinced it is accurate or productive. I may write something on that alone, but I understand why the allure, and that's not plain anti-Semitism.

However, and this is when I may become unsavoury to some readers, there is anti-Semitism on the left, there always has been, and sometimes it disguises itself as 'merely' critique of Israel. The self-defined international left (by which I refer to, by and large, the American and European & British left, because that's how they see themselves—as 'international left'—a problem in and of itself) has had an anti-Semitism problem which each Jewish author on the left I ever read has ever pointed out. As some of you may know, for my sins I have written a biography of Rosa Luxemburg, who had written, formally and informally, on anti-Semitism around her. The Jewess most often taken to be the symbol of internationalism and the 'no borders' trope had still been a victim of racism. Because racism targets you for who you are, and not what you think.

There are many discourses doing the rounds right now that are plainly anti-Semitic. They are not often being called out. When you're in your lefty group and someone says something that doesn't sound decent, and you're not directly implicated, you might find it hard or lack the motivation to call it out. As I had written here yesterday, some of the accounts of the massacre of 7th October were reeking of anti-Semitism. Denying victims' voices, abuse of their memory such as tearing down posters of the kidnapped and spreading conspiracy theories about the day itself.

On a personal note, I had never felt completely safe when I lived in the UK. Perhaps it is ironic that I write this while living during an actual war and have missiles thrown at me twice daily, but I feel safer here. There is a part of me that toys with the idea of writing a memoir of being a Jewish Israeli on the ranks of the radical British left. I always second-guessed conversations around me and motivations of people talking to me.

So, now we get to action points. This is the first time I've thought of something that resembles an action point if you're going on marches this week and/or encouraging others to go.

1. In addition to demanding a ceasefire, if you are marching to protest the targeting of civilians, please make part of your demands to release the hostages. Please make sure that if you're calling to safeguard the well-being of civilians in the midst of a war, it means *all* civilians. Otherwise you're not advocating human rights but revenge.

2. And this is a direct consequence of what I wrote above. If you encounter anti-Semitism on the marches, please call it out. For one, it won't help the Palestinian cause. It's true that Israel is weaponisng anti-Semitism in order to defend its actions but you have to *have* anti-Semitism in order to weaponise it. So it is up to you, reader, to make these marches about liberation and human rights and not about revenge and counter-victimisation. This means calling out revenge on Palestinians as a policy (which trust me, we on the Israeli left have been doing since day one and is crucial and urgent) *but* also calling out taking down posters of victims and hate speech in the marches. This is not 'whataboutism'. But it is about human rights.

## Many fires everywhere; while all eyes on Gaza

I say this in all cautiousness necessary, if there is one area in which there is a very present danger for genocidal violence, it's the West Bank. I'm going to write a little bit about what's happening in the West Bank and then on the crackdown on Palestinian–Israeli rights within Israel.

The strange reality of being an Israeli lefty is that you constantly tell the world that things are both worse and better than they think. Or, at least different. Shifting against populism and hyperbolic speech (I understand well its political efficacy, but it does have a political price, of normalisation and habituation of discourse), a quest for accuracy, for relying on empirical data and harking back to international law is my and my human rights community comrades' primary motivation. This means that for the hard international left we are too mellow, and for the Israeli mainstream we are "'traitors who wash dirty laundry abroad". A term that always comes to my mind is from Kafka's masterwork *The Castle*, "not from the castle and not from the village".

Over the past years, Israel has accelerated a policy of de facto annexation. Under the Trump presidency, there was a plan to legally (de jure) annex the West Bank, make apartheid the de facto system there. I remind the readers that apartheid is a crime against humanity, and many, including Michael Sfard, Human Rights Watch, B'tselem and Amnesty have shown persuasively that at the very least, there is apartheid in the West Bank and East Jerusalem. Most accounts now also see the whole of Israel between the river and the sea as enacting apartheid. Anyway, a few words of explanation on settlements, outposts and why this is a crucial time to keep your eyes on the West Bank in particular.

All settlements are illegal according to international law, as they amount to transferring civilian population into an occupied territory. Israel has devised a system of legislation which applies only in Israeli law yet is a way to at least monitor settlement expansion. There are at least 700,000 settlers in the West Bank, some living in cities such as Modi'in Ilit and Beitar Ilit, or Ariel. Some settlers, especially new immigrants to Israel, live there out of economic considerations; when Israel pushed for expansion of settlements it had made them far cheaper than flats within the Green Line. At the same time, there are illegal outposts (I am using local terminology to remind that *all* settlements are illegal). These are often ad hoc outposts that do not comply with the Israeli legal system. Very often they are founded by land grabs and 'facts on the ground', Palestinians waking up one day and finding out their land had been occupied by settlers. These are clearly ideologically motivated. They are often in the midst of Palestinian villages, meant to create a wedge within Palestinian continuity, at a high risk to the settlers. Rather than the state of Israel doing what any reasonable state would do, saying: if you want to go and occupy a foreign land, do it at your own expense, the Israeli army puts in ample resources into securing those outposts. More often than not, soldiers who are ideologically aligned with the settlers' agenda of expansion at the expense of Palestinian continuity and culture find themselves guarding these outposts, creating a perfect storm to make Palestinians' lives completely precarious and unbearable.

I want to write a little bit about settler violence. There has been a lot of discussion of that, with the Israeli centre-right keen to present them as 'a few bad apples', unhinged radicals acting on their own agenda. However, data collated by NGOs (especially Yesh Din and B'tselem), have shown a strong correlation between settlement expansion and legalisation of these outposts and this violence. Meaning, this is a way settlers gain control of land, scare off Palestinians, very often with the full guardianship and while the Israeli army is watching. This allows Israel formally to acquire land in the West Bank aided by settler violence, without adhering even to the minimal accountability it had set itself as a benchmark.

Over the past month, the process of expulsion, amounting to ethnic cleansing in several areas in the West Bank: South Hebron Hills, for instance, has been accelerated. The settlers know well that the Israeli government, as well as the world at large, is busy looking at Gaza, and so it is their moment to increase violence, deterrence and fear so that Palestinians find it impossible to stay in their homes.

Israel has been operating for years in a policy of separation between the West Bank and Gaza, to eliminate any Palestinian solidarity and possibility for an independent state. There is an alignment of local and international factors that induce deliberate killing, such as today in Jenin, to destroy any Palestinian presence in the West Bank. And so, I say this with caution and knowledge of facts on the ground, keep raising what's happening in the West Bank and keep your eyes firmly there.

At the same time, in Israel itself, as always during increased militarisation, Palestinian citizens of Israel, who are 20% of the population, are suffering increased attacks either formally, such as illegally firing Palestinians for supposedly 'terrorist support' on social media, or informally, such as everyday harassment of various magnitude, and an atmosphere of a racist witch hunt which makes everyday life nearly impossible. It is currently impossible to protest against the war, for instance. Even for Jews it is dangerous, but Palestinians are arrested if they dare publicly challenge Israeli policies in Gaza.

Against these horrors described above, I can share many stories of Israeli/Palestinian partnership which commits to safety through solidarity. Thus far, there have been many instances of Israeli–Palestinian solidarity despite incessant attempts by the far-right government to create lynching in the street and to have citizens taking the law into their own hands. One such worrying trend has been easing the conditions for acquiring weapons, which my American readers know, never ends well. Yet there has been strong resistance on the street and refusal to sink back into what happened in May 2021, that huge surge of violence in mixed Israeli/Palestinian cities. This speaks a lot to anti-racist organising efforts, and there have been many clandestine acts of support and defence on a one-to-one basis. It is hell on earth being a Palestinian citizen of Israel right now. I don't pretend to really know what it feels like, but I do know there have been beautiful acts of solidarity and I pray with all my might that they develop and expand. Standing Together, a movement that focuses on Jewish-Palestinian solidarity within Israel, hosted some joint gatherings and comrades in the leadership there tell me they were completely full. Rabbis for Human Rights is organising joint

Jewish-Palestinian olive harvests in order to challenge settler violence in the West Bank. So, in the light of all the grim information above, if you'd like to see change on the ground, follow and support those of us who are trying to fight from within, and keep yours eyes firmly on all that is happening here. Many fires everywhere can either catch each other and become one huge fire that cannot be put out, or can be put out individually. I hope you join in the latter quest for human rights for all between the river and the sea.

10.11.2023

## All of the Guineas, no one wins in wars, or fighting for shared humanity (but against moral equivocation)

Yesterday I heard of another person I know killed in Gaza. A cousin of a former comrade at Peace Now. She wrote to me, "our sadness is endless". Week five of the war.

Today I went to a reading group at my favourite independent book store, Sipur Pashut, named for an Agnon short story. Today's discussion was led by brilliant writer Orna Coussin who shared her essay: 'More than *Three Guineas*, or only feminism will prevent the (next) war'. It was a lively discussion and the essay gave me much to chew about, as did returning to *Three Guineas* which I did last night.

Cheered and inspired I got on my bus home, and suddenly, my phone went—alarm (we have an application that notifies us of alarms, in addition to the actual alarm). We didn't hear alarms outside of the bus so there was a short debate what to do. The bus driver stopped and we all ran off the bus. A family with two young children found a little hideaway to go. I threw myself, face down, on the pavement as we have been instructed to do when caught outdoors during a rocket barrage. Very audible bangs were heard, and we could see the tail of the missile in the sky.

I got up, crossed the road, and as the street was filling up again I caught another bus home. My knees were shaking. I couldn't really speak. I texted my mum and aunt to say I was OK and en route home. When I got home I realised I had got my period, a few days early. Two women were injured in Tel Aviv from this attack, from pieces of the missile that had hit them when they were hiding.

If I dare share something like this on social media, the response is quick to come. What about Gaza? Do you not know how many people died by *your* fire today? Do you know how many children *you* have killed? How dare you complain?

And I want to tell you, no one wins in wars, and no one is really safe. This is also a response to the 'keep safe' wish, given earnestly but a bit empty considering. No one benefits from these rounds of violence. Now, I feel it necessary to say the explicit. Of course I do not equate myself with the suffering of the people in Gaza. I have a phone app that warns me and counter–missiles operations. And my army is indiscriminately bombing civilian populations. I am well aware of that. But let me tell you, comrades, being in 'the safe and liberal and privileged Tel Aviv' isn't fun these days either.

Going back to Virginia Woolf was a good excuse to revisit my favourite paragraph in *Three Guineas*, in which she suggests using a match to burn down college and start anew (Bryant and May, no less! a small nod to the Matchwomen's Strike, such a significant but historical instance of what happens when women organise).

I've increasingly felt the need to restart discussion around war, around *this* war, around Israel/Palestine. I feel we need to get back to defending shared humanity. Not by glossing over power divisions and privilege, but by repeating, ad infinitum, that no one wins in wars. Departing from moral equivocation, that fact that I am miserable doesn't justify what my country is doing in Gaza, nor that this war can be justified, nor contradicts the very obvious fact that the people in Gaza are suffering more than I do. This only means, once more, that no one wins in wars.

I feel like trying to gear up all of the *Guineas*—all of the resources poured into discussion around what's happening here and just stating, again and again. No one wins in wars. There are only losers. They are losing in differing magnitudes (once again, away from moral equivocation) but we are all losing. All of the time. I feel like if only I had all of the *Guineas* and could start anew, come together around shared humanity and against the violence of all sides, maybe things would be different.

Shabbat shalom—a Shabbat of peace.


11.11.2023

Ahead of the protests today: why aren't
Israelis protesting the war? (or aren't they?):
State of fascism and protest in Israel

I hope all marches pass peacefully today. I am also praying that the rightful call for a ceasefire and protection of civilians in Gaza is coupled by a demand to return Israeli hostages held by Hamas (if you are marching to protect citizens, this is an obvious call).

I thought this is a good time to write a little about what's happening here vis-a-vis protest, why dynamics are as they are, and predict how things might unfold.

The war cut abruptly one of the most interesting and impressive protest movements in Israeli history. Since January 2023, rain (there's a famous photograph of tens of thousands protesting in the pouring rain, holding umbrellas) or shine (trust me, protesting in 40 degrees Celsius isn't fun either, and that happened too) millions of Israelis went every week, sometimes several times a week, to demand that Netanyahu leaves his seat and stop the judicial overhaul (at attempt to intervene in the authority of the Supreme Court and pass more authority to Israel's most right-wing government, something that is still ongoing). This was a truly singular and unique moment and it didn't seem to be ending.

This mainstream protest movement did not really challenge the state of occupation. Indeed, Netanyahu's legacy is first and foremost to normalise "managing the conflict", deepening occupation and apartheid while taking any possible discussion of a political resolution, peace or a difference from the status quo— moving towards full annexation—out of public discourse. However, as part of this protest there was a solid anti-occupation bloc of which I have been part. I also had the honour to address this bloc twice: speaking specifically on Gaza and the need to end the siege and protect the 2.2 million civilians who live there. This bloc changed in size and prominence in the main protest; I recall two instances in which it grew, the last attack on Gaza in May

2023, as well as the settler pogrom in Huwara, in which settlers killed one Palestinian, injured over 100 and left huge devastation in the town. Many of us persevered in this bloc realising that the mainstream discourse has, once again thanks to Netanyahu and his cronies, disabled any discussion of Palestinian human rights or an end to the occupation. The main theme under which many organisations and individuals came together was 'no democracy with occupation'.

Once again, 7th October changed everything; not least, stopped this protest movement that seemed like it wasn't stopping..

Many of the protest organisations have stepped up to take the Israeli state's failure to care for its citizens; to cook, to care, to organise for the internally displaced, for reserve soldiers, for their families and communities at home, and to cook for many shivas, sometimes consequently, sometimes for multiple family members at once. This civil society-run operation is truly astounding and shows just how low the Israeli state has sunk, pushing monies towards the settler lobby and the ultra-orthodox while starving any viable emergency responses. The main efforts in terms of public advocacy have been, and this is across the board, politically, the call to bring back the hostages. It is clear to all around the world that this is not a priority for Netanyahu. Thus, once again civil society is taking the government's place.

A word on Netanyahu. His popularity in polls is sinking, even within his own electorate. The only call to keep him where he is now is due to a worry that it would weaken Israel's position amidst a war, but even that is a minority. A majority of Israelis think he has to go, and the sooner the better. For Netanyahu, political life after this horrific time will probably end. I type this with all caution necessary. This is a man who has survived many times in which he *should* have been unseated, and yet now, I say cautiously, it seems even his own electorate thinks he has to go. This also means sadly Netanyahu is gaining support for the continuation of the war, thus has little interest to end it; even his supporters will demand he goes after the war ends.

Incidentally, it's my birthday in three weeks; I'll turn forty-two. I spent my sixteenth birthday protesting against Netanyahu when he first gained power. Do the math.

Anyway, back to public responses to the war. There are interesting trends to observe. The call to return all hostages is pretty much undisputed. Among the families of those taken hostage are some (not many, but some) Netanyahu supporters. After a few clashes in the early weeks of the protest between those protesting Netanyahu and the hostages' families there is now a spatial and temporal division so that these two calls are distinct. It is also significant to say here that much of the public gathering around these issues is done in the same place where many of the anti-government protests took place, Kaplan Street, opposite the Israeli Ministry of Defense. On the other hand, many of the bereaved families are raising their voice against Netanyahu, saying very harsh things such as that the blood of their loved ones is on Netanyahu's hands.

So, the protest movement calling for Netanyahu and the entire government to resign is growing in numbers and strength.

A splinter of this protest against Netanyahu, which has started small but is growing in numbers too, is the call for a ceasefire and protecting all civilians. I was present in one of this movement's first organising meetings. The growing fascism in Israel and political persecution in various ways—Palestinian citizens of Israel are often arrested for Facebook posts, for showing compassion towards people in Gaza, or even just for alluding to the Palestinian flag. Israeli Jews are of course more privileged but are not safe either. A teacher was arrested (he is still held in custody now) and his house violated and searched due to his show of compassion to citizens killed in Gaza. A friend of mine texted me discreetly and told me she was questioned for seven hours for her Instagram posts.

I've been cautious online but I guess one day my time will come too.

Add to that very violent streets, both police and right-wingers who are looking to enact violence on *anyone* daring to contest the necessity of the Israeli strategy. The conditions for carrying arms have been eased, so many fascists are now carrying guns.

I don't think Israeli Jews, even leftists, are the victims. We are part of the hegemony and I write from the wrong side of history. However I want to answer the question motivating this essay: why aren't we protesting the war, like you, in London, New York or Berlin?

First, I want to state a non-ideological but obvious reason. It is scary to stand outside and protest when missiles fall where you are. Many people who used to come and protest in Tel Aviv are scared to do so.

Second, and crucially, I want to write something about where we are emotionally. In Jewish faith the thirty days after a loved one dies are considered the most intense period of mourning, but then actual grieving starts. We are a society very much processing what has happened to us. Everyone is implicated; whether knowing someone who died, who has been kidnapped, a survivor or someone who has been internally displaced. More often than not we know all of the above. So our first and foremost call is to bring our fellow citizens back.

In addition, of course, there is the growing fascism I wrote about. I am lucky and privileged, working in a sector that won't penalise me if I go to protest, living a very safe life, but this is not true of all Israelis. So there is a price to pay for raising one's voice, *even* just calling for a ceasefire.

I feel and think the movement to protest the war and calling for a ceasefire will grow. This is a natural consequence and, knowing the organisational atmosphere here, it is already happening and likely to expand. I am happy to report I've been at all these protests and they were fairly safe, with only a few right-wingers calling us traitors.

And then, all organisers know, that once the war ends, a ceasefire is called and/or reserve duty soldiers are back home, the magnitude of the protest here will be unprecedented. Many of us: middle class, liberal, (privileged) citizens are bearing the brunt of the state's failings, of it catering to Jewish supremacy instead of the safety of all—Jews and Palestinians.

Being an Israeli lefty is hard in many ways but I love my community which has always sustained me and inspired me. So keep an eye on what's happening here. We are already not silent and we are done with being used as pawns and sacrificed for bloodythirsty politicians.

## Al Shifa hospital and the morality of the Israeli attack on Gaza

I'm on my period, for the second time this war. Women reading this : you will know this adds anxiety, being more tetchy than usual, fatigue and just feeling like shit. This also means for me this war has been going on for more than a month. It makes me feel the passing of time very viscerally.

One thing I've noticed, even within my own thinking, but certainly in general arguments around the war, that there has been a conflation of political, strategic, legal, moral and other justifications (or lack of) for this war. The Israeli army repeats ad infinitum that Hamas has been using the civilian population as human shields. The Israeli army has been known to lie. This may well be the case again. However, it may also be at least partially true. This, by the way, may be either intentional or unintentional: as I've written here before the Gaza Strip is very densely populated thus civilians being part of the military locations could be or might not be a matter of policy choice. In any case this implicates only the strategic justification for the war. The political justification for the war, ie whether there is an overarching support for the war locally within Israel or internationally, hinges upon but is also distinct from the strategic justification for war. Public opinion and justification to fight a war hinges of course on the strategic argument but is also independent from it. But today

I would like to focus on the moral justification, or lack of it, for this war.

First, I want to write about something I have been considering. We all, as human beings, pass moral judgments on issues in which we are either implicated or not. White people have moral judgments on racism (and how to combat it). Men have opinions on the right to life or the right to abortion. I believe, especially as a Jewish human rights scholar and activist, that we are all implicated in judgments made on issues that either relate to us directly or not at all. If it weren't for this inter-human morality no lessons would be learnt from the wars and horrors of the past. But we are glad that some lessons have been learnt. However, this brings me to the second point.

I believe, with all my might, that having existential distance from an issue does not deny having moral judgement about it, nor the justification to express that judgement, or better access to moral judgement of the issue at hand. I am not of the 'no uterus, no opinion' camp, nor do I think white people should abstain from talking about racism. Again, when it comes to Israel/Palestine, one can talk of degrees of implications (ie European or American citizens who feel they would like control over their tax money). But clearly, thinking of the above examples, being directly implicated in these issues, having very specific existential stakes in the war, does not deny the right to moral judgement (or, in fact, thinking of these examples, perhaps even validates that right).

I have been thinking a lot of the distinctness of the moral argument from others for the past few weeks since it has been known that Israel is bombing hospitals in Gaza. This has made me feel chilled to my bone. For context: this is, of course, a war crime. Many war crimes have been committed by all sides in this war, so it is not enough to say that.

I am indifferent at this point to whether the Israeli army is correct or is lying. It may well be true that Hamas is stashing weapons under the hospital. For the sake of the argument, I am accepting this as an underlying assumption. And still, I want to say: I do not consent morally to having my voice used to justify this action. Even if it is politically, strategically and perhaps even legally, one proves that Hamas was the first to harm Gazan civilians, this does not justify Israel's actions morally. I do not consent to my country's actions in the Gaza Strip from a moral point of view. It is clear that Israel cannot completely eradicate Hamas in the Gaza Strip. I will write at some point some possible scenarios to arise out of this war. But if the cost necessary to defend me is this disproportionate and inhumane direct targeting of civilians, then we will have to pay the security price. It will be heavy, but so be it.

I do want to again make the point that of course morality is never absolute, hence a lot of these arguments are lost on social media. Civilians are consistently targeted on both sides. This is not only a war crime, but a moral crime. Yet, I believe strongly that even in a war that has clearly crossed many moral lines, it is imperative to draw a line and say: this is too far.

Perhaps this is why for the first time I went with a sign that I had made to the anti-war demonstration yesterday. I wrote three messages: Ceasefire now. Bring the hostages back. Netanyahu out.

I care about safeguarding the safety of the people in the Gaza Strip. I also care about my people and my well-being. I equally care about our morality here as Israelis. I also think, once again, moral arguments are different when one has a stake in this war. If I am wrong, and the Israeli army is right, and the missiles under al Shifa hospital are the next missile barrages thrown on Tel Aviv, I will be paying the price for my mistake. But my moral judgement does not change as it is not contingent upon the strategic or political justification for this action.

I return in my mind to John Donne's beautiful poem, though please bear in mind this above discussion the next time you moralise with an Israeli/Palestinian.

No man is an island entire of itself; every man is a piece of the continent, a part of the main; if a clod be washed away by the sea, Europe is the less, as well as if a promontory were, as well as any manner of thy friends or of thine own were; any man's death diminishes me, because I am involved in mankind. And therefore never send to know for whom the bell tolls; it tolls for thee.

14.11.2023

Discussed: "There is not path to peace, peace is the path": In memory of Vivian Silver z"l

Today we woke up to the news that it had been confirmed that Vivian Silver was killed by Hamas militants on 7th October. We had assumed that she was kidnapped to Gaza. She was texting with her son on the 7th October: "there are terrorists in my house". Then they lost contact.

I am mainly thinking of her sons and her entire family today.

But, the murder of Vivian Silver makes all of us peace and human rights activists in Israel/Palestine bereft today. My social media feeds are full of her beaming smile, and I can't remember ever seeing her not smiling. It's a testimony to who she was that so many people, Israeli and Palestinian both, and so many organisations are grieving for her today.

But I want to write about Vivian's spirit, *ruach*, as we say in Hebrew, and the calling she has left us. For me, her senseless, heinous murder at the age of seventy-four is a calling to avenge it by advocating for peace with more determination.

In all Saturday evening protests against Netanyahu there were always older women, clad in turquoise scarves, shouting: woman, peace, equality, social justice. The women of Women Wage Peace (It is an excellent pun in Hebrew, as the verb for waving hello is the same as 'waging peace') were there, every week. Vivian was one of the pillars of the group. She really lived the ethos of the movement, that we cannot live in this land without peace, and without giving more voice to women. She was also a founder and active in numerous Israeli–Palestinian coexistence organisations, and especially worked with Bedouin communities in the Negev/Naqab.

Vivian chose to live in Be'eri, not far from Gaza. There is something important concerning so many peace and human rights activists, kidnapped, killed or affected by the 7th October attacks. You should understand. The people who chose to live around Gaza, especially, did so as they knew there was no other way than to live together. They understood life in Gaza well especially, those who had come, like Vivian, long before the siege.

They knew Gazans and had wished to make a bridge, not build up a wall. When asked in an interview what she wishes for her grandchildren she said "that they have Palestinian friends". She had said recently that we need to work for a political resolution as we cannot proceed from one round of violence to another.

She also fought to have more women in decision-making positions. She knew that women could counter many violent, dangerous decisions made by men.

Over the past weeks I have found myself connecting to many women around me who knew and loved Vivian. Many women, especially from my generation and younger, and myself, feel like we have failed Vivian and her generation. We have been talking to each other a lot today. We have to continue to advocate for a just peace. That is the only solution for all of us living between the river and the sea.

I want to write something about this word, peace. Thirty-eight days into this horrific war, with more than 11,000 Palestinians killed and the Israeli death toll rising by the day, it feels like this endless, senseless violence is becoming more and more merely the crystallisation of the rage of the Israeli leadership and army, who clearly don't have a plan but revenge through mass displacement, killings, ethnic cleansing in our name.

The word peace is what we need now. Not just to shout big words and to make the message more radical to the ear. Not using legal terms we hardly understand. But to demand just peace. A just peace.

When I was the director of Peace Now I hated the word peace in our title. It was hard to carry. In times without fighting it felt old-fashioned, a memory from a world no longer here. It felt like hope we didn't deserve to have. How dare we speak of peace when there is so much injustice done in our name? As a lefty Israeli I disliked it more by the day.

But, during the May 2021 attack on Gaza I felt proud of the name. Suddenly, it made sense to me. The only thing we need to demand is a just peace. Not to shy away from the past and its injustices, but always look into the future. How futile it feels to me to be stuck in endless conversations that had no horizon, no outlook. All of us here, between the river and the sea, deserve not only justice but also peace. We must continue to demand it.

Among her other activities (she was, among other things, on the board of Israeli human rights NGO, B'tselem), Vivian volunteered to drive medical patients from the Gaza border to Israeli hospitals. Amidst Israel's cruel permit regime medical patients got, at times, permission to seek medical treatment outside of the Gaza Strip. My cousin also volunteered with this organisation and activity. I mention this as Vivian knew people from Gaza, first hand. She trusted them. She drove them in her car, alone, to get them to the hospital they had needed to reach.

I wish for all of us, the peace and human rights community she has left behind, to work hard to rebuild this trust between all of us, Israelis and Palestinians living all across the land. To trust each other as people and as peoples. To see the better in each other and not the worse. To look at each other not with trauma but with hope for a different future. I feel that this would be the only way to avenge this horrific loss of Vivian's life, that will hurt many for a long time.

Rest in power, Vivian Silver z"l. You have taught us so much, and could have taught us much more. To honour your memory we need to walk in your path. There is no path to peace; peace *is* the path.

## The ethics and aesthetics of death

It has been a strange and sad week. The images from Gaza are overwhelmingly awful. Personally, I keep getting news of yet another connection to someone who was killed in the fighting in Gaza, another person who was assumed hostage but was found dead. The air is thick with grief. The feeling of loss and anxious waiting is everywhere. Whenever we hear of a soldier who was killed I have this thought circling in my mind: Oh god I hope it's not anyone I know. These are young men and women, from my circles, in their 20s, 30s... But is it less sad if it's not someone I know? At this point we've all supported someone grieving, lost someone who we know personally. We are all grieving. Yet. Still. Continuously and without an end in sight.

The first ever funeral I attended was for one of my soldiers when I was in the Israeli army. (I was a Hebrew teacher to Russian immigrants to Israel during my army service). One warm Saturday night, I was sitting with my parents outside. Suddenly my officer called. There had been a bombing attack. Our soldier, Diez Normanov, was killed. What happened after was weeks and months of trying to work through this with his classmates, with our staff, with ourselves.

The death toll in Gaza is approaching 12,000. These are incomprehensible numbers. Whole families dead. No one left to mourn. It is just impossible to imagine, and yet, we must, exactly because of this impossibility.

I have been thinking, especially since this war, more than many which had come before it, has been really unravelling on social media.

A few thoughts from the Israeli side. Traditionally, and historically, Israeli media does not display gory images of slain bodies. First, there is always concern for the feelings of the families. Secondly, and crucially, in Jewish faith we do not observe our dead. We do not hold open casket funerals. Once a person dies, we do not watch their body. Thus showing mutilated bodies would not only be disrespectful to the families, but also to the dead person's faith. If they are Jewish, of course. On the 7th there were casualties of a variety of faiths.

Thirdly, and this is relevant to our current moment, it has taken a tremendously long time to secure identification of the victims of the 7th October. The bodies were mutilated so badly, sometimes literally burnt to the ground, that it has been hard to find remains and confirm identification. A friend who lost a family member on the 7th told me they were called several times to give DNA samples, as several false identifications had to be ruled out.

I have seen some speculation internationally about the death toll in Israel. It feels especially offensive that not only do we suffer this hideous period of waiting to confirm whether our relatives and loved ones are dead, this confusion, related to the way they were murdered, is then used as a 'gotcha!' argument showing that

Israel is lying. As I write here often, I have no doubt at all that the Israeli army and Israeli state lie. But, in this case, after supporting people who had to directly face up to this reality of uncertainty and hard wait, it feels especially gruesome to deal with this discourse.

Over to Gaza, where graphic images of armless children, bloody corpses piling up, and children being pulled from under the rubble are populating our social media feeds. It feels hideous beyond words to perceive this, to have to witness this horrific massacre, unreasonable in magnitude. Whatever Israeli forces are intending to achieve in Gaza, nothing can justify this. But beyond the strong moral opposition to being party to such a massacre, it feels unbearably depressing that Palestinians have been so dehumanised that they have to show their dead bodies, in thousands, to get any kind of traction from the international community. As I have written here in the past, I had worked in advocacy focused on Gaza, and outside of these hideous attacks it was very hard to garner interest in Gaza. With the West Bank constantly inflamed, the world's attention was always elsewhere. Moreover, images of joy, of life, of survival despite the siege, rarely did the rounds on social media. The world doesn't want or can't engage living Palestinians. They will only provide them a moment when they become corpses, buried under rubble. The pressure to stop Israel's siege is non-existent outside of times of war.

It feels that the need to constantly engage physical proof, gory images, to showcase mutilated bodies is to accept the world's dehumanisation of victims. Israel decided to show, in closed screenings to select audiences, some footage from 7th October to counter disinformation and conspiracy theories around that awful day. It feels that one thing that binds Israelis and Palestinians together is that the world doesn't engage us until we are dead, and we can prove we are dead.

When there is a school shooting in the USA, arguably also a highly politicised issue, the media shows photos of victims and sombre memorials. No one doubts the body count or that the shooting existed until you witness a picture of a half-disintegrated body.

As with everything in this war, there is no parity. These are not two equal sides. The Israeli death toll, when it is finally confirmed, is bound to be lower than the Palestinian one considering the size and strength of the Israeli army compared to resources at the disposal of the Palestinian fighters. But yet, at the same time, we all have to show our dead to the world in order to win an argument.

When Diez was killed, I was asked to give the eulogy. I had just turned nineteen. His mother had arrived from the former USSR, after not seeing him for years. I will never forget the image of her sobbing on his grave. When someone dies, a family is broken. Israeli attacks on Gaza are erasing a whole culture. We are here constantly shifting from one moment of horror to another, from sinking in one iteration of grief to another. And yes, many of us Israelis too are horrified by the images coming out of Gaza, even if we are also grieving for our own friends and families. At the end of the day, one thing that has shifted in me is that I care much less for what the world will think of me and my grief, especially when directly supporting those who had lost loved ones over the past six weeks. I will not perform my grief to you so that you believe me. If you choose not to believe me, that is your choice.

Equally, I pray, hope and work for a day in which the world will be able to engage Palestinians when they are alive, thriving, celebrating, and not only when they are killed in thousands. This is the cause that I work for, humanity and dignity in life, not only in death.

18.11.2023

## My speech in Israel's first authorised demonstration (against the war, to bring back all hostages and for peace)

Up till now, it's been illegal to organise protests and demonstrations. The police and army authorities used a range of excuses: from security (though, large gatherings and vigils for the hostages contradict that) to saying that calling for a ceasefire in the midst of a war is incitement. On Thursday evening, after a long legal battle that reached the Israeli Supreme Court, the first demonstration was authorised. On Friday my friend Noa Levy, Hadash Tel Aviv chair (Hadash is the Israeli–Palestinian socialist party) rang and asked if I was willing to speak. I said of course, yes.

When arriving at the protest I was confused at first. There was a massive counter-protest. I don't know which was larger but the counter-protest was very loud. Lots of Israeli flags and random shouts against us. The demonstration was heavily policed: at the entrance to the protest the police looked at each and every sign to approve its messaging and confiscated some which they didn't like. It was bizarre. During the protest itself the counter-protesters did everything they could to disrupt us, including cutting off electricity (we switched to megaphones), shouting loudly beside the speakers (the police didn't say anything and just watched) but we made it, with more shouting than usual.

I thought I'd share with you my speech today. Some sentences work better in Hebrew.

Stop the war. Stop the massacre in Gaza.

It's been six weeks since our hearts were broken. The pain only intensifies, but with time we gain clarity too.

We will not be quiet and not rest until we return each and every one of the hostages to us. We demand a prisoner exchange deal now. We will not be silent in the face of evil, of incitement and division. We are being turned one against each other. We will not be silent against the fascist hunting of dissenters, especially Palestinian citizens of Israel. We will not be silent when our friends are hunted down, persecuted, fired from their jobs. We will not be silent when our freedom of expression is abused.

We demand a ceasefire now. We demand to stop the massacre in Gaza. We demand a stop to harming civilians. We demand a stop to those images of children buried under the rubble. I say: not in my name! In Gaza and in Sderot* children want to live. Stop the massacre in Gaza.

This week we lost a great voice in the peace and human rights camp. Vivian Silver z"l taught many of us that we have no choice but to demand a political solution. We must demand that women lead political

*a Southern town targeted by Hamas

decisions as only women can get us out of this circle of vengeance and cruelty. We must insist on a just peace, a sustainable peace, peace without oppression and occupation, peace without a cruel closure which for seventeen years denies freedom of movement of 2.2 million people, peace between equals, peace between all with equal human rights between the river and the sea.

I will end on Vivian's words: there is no path to peace, peace is the path.

The speech was well received (apart from fascists making noise!). I was honoured to be speaking alongside Hadash Member of Knesset Aida Touma-Suleiman who was expelled from the Knesset for objecting to the war, Sami Abu Shehadeh (former Balad member of Knesset) and the amazing Maoz Inon, who lost both his parents in the 7th October Massacres.

I got home for a bit, and then went to the weekly vigil for the hostages. It was sadder and smaller than usual; there had been a large march to the Knesset of the hostages' families, so the vigil was dedicated to abducted children as the International Day for the Rights of the Child is on 20th November.

As I walked home, I realised how exhausted I was of it all; not only physically but also emotionally. The past few weeks really taught me to harden my heart, perhaps not a bad skill for life. I have been immersing myself in the evidence, both images from Gaza as well as testimonies from the 7th October. In addition, I'm tired of being a token Jew/token Israeli supporting peoples' political processes from afar/entertaining hypothetical moral dilemmas which to me/us are not hypothetical at all. I am deep in survival mode, and between caring for my family and getting through each day, each day feels anew like a challenge. We have no idea how long this will last. We are all at the end of our tether. Never have I felt more urgency for peace.

19.11.2023

## Women in war

This strange period and its abundant exhaustion also gives rise to me an immense feeling of gratitude for things I sometimes take for granted and which sustain me. In my speech yesterday I made the point that women should be brought to the frontline of decisions, of negotiations, in all discourses. I had thought of Vivian Silver z"l, but also of Aida Thouma-Suleiman who was speaking before me. If there was something that I felt made me come to the protest and speaking worthwhile, was the ability to give her a hug beforehand. Working in politics here enabled me to meet first hand my longstanding sheroes. Aida has not only been a voice for integrity and moral courage, she's always been a wonderful person to work with; precise, humble, and warm to younger women.

One of the things I'm most grateful for on the Israeli–Palestinian left is having strong women to derive inspiration and strength from, to turn to for advice, and to get a solidarity hug in demonstrations when I needed it the most. Since I came back here nearly three years ago I've been blown away by the kindness of women towards me, especially older women who had been trailblazers for me, who had worked so that I had possibilities to choose from that I took for granted (or not), who had sometimes paid hefty prices for this path they had made for us.

I am also grateful to all of those who continue to engage in structural analysis which pushes us to think longer and harder about who pays the heftiest price for patriarchy: those women who already are marginalised and oppressed, those women who experience most racism, poverty and other forms of exclusion.

I am not a liberal feminist and am not an essentialist. I don't think we are all potential mothers, whose kindness and soft heart will counter the male traits so affluent in politics. But men have made such a mess of this world, we might as well have a go at fixing it. And perhaps the fact that we have had to struggle this long against patriarchy means that we have skills, pragmatism and perseverance that they lack.

Things are not always rainbows and unicorns between women, of course, and perhaps it's especially disappointing to see women unkind to other women. I had suffered a lot of sexism in this line of work, including from women. One memorable moment was a telling-off call from a female member of the board I worked with during International Women's Month a few years ago, telling me I'm not nice enough to the board. In that period I worked 10–12 hours per day, if you're a feminist and reading this you know how exhausting March is, with extra commitments added to day-to-day obligations. I am grateful to a male feminist friend, who I called after that call, exhausted and exasperated, for him to say to me that this is the classic "you should smile more" chat. This is also the place to say I have endless gratitude to feminist men, trans people and non-binary comrades who have helped me in so many ways, who have supported me, and who see sexism when

I might miss it. Sometimes when I/we women don't see it, because if we spotted it all the time we would go crazy.

This period also makes me feel the need to tell these women in my life who had shaped my thinking, and are struggling in this war as well, how much I appreciate them. To offer a cup of coffee, glass of wine or a chat, and to do what I can to support them. Most had lived through the Yom Kippur war in 1973, the biggest trauma for all apart from this one. I feel that my generation—I'll be 42 in a week and a half—is here to bring up the younger generation while supporting the older one. We are nourished by dual inspiration. The younger feminist activists here never cease to amaze me, and I have the knowledge and experience of older feminists to fall back on. So this is something I'm doing at the moment, actively and intentionally, supporting and elevating women and other non-male voices around me.

And so, this morning I woke up, despite the violence at the demonstration and mixed feelings about everything, with an overwhelming sense of gratitude: for the women here who sustain me at the moment, and specifically for the immense privilege to speak after Aida Thouma-Souleiman, and to give her a solidarity hug.

23.11.2023

### And waiting is so very hard/ bring them all back

I am just back in Tel Aviv after spending a few days with my mother, out of town. There have been no missiles thus far where she is and I pray this continues. I notice my anxiety reducing substantially when I leave town, able to take showers without worrying about an alarm, and generally relaxing a bit more.

Yesterday it was announced that a hostage swap deal will take place alongside a four-day ceasefire. It was meant to start today and is already postponed to tomorrow.

The deal is supposed to include swapping fifty people, mainly children and women, in exchange for convicted Palestinian prisoners held in Israeli prisons. This isn't as straightforward as it sounds. Some Palestinians convicted of "terrorism" are those who called to throw stones at the Israeli army. On the other hand, it's unclear if captured female soldiers, most of whom are twenty years old, will be included in the deal. I'm not going into the international law distinctions between citizen and combatant here, but if you have a daughter, think of her at twenty, or remember yourself at twenty; these are some of the women whose return we await.

It is hard to describe the extent to which the entire country rallies around the hostages. It is essential to go back to some of the basic details of the 7th October. These are citizens pulled out of their beds on a Saturday morning and abruptly abducted. We are unsure whether they even know that there's an ongoing war, or whether they know others had been taken hostage, including some of their own families. We don't know where they are held, whether they are held together. Hamas says some have been held captive by the Islamic Jihad. Some are apparently held by ordinary Gazans.

The trauma of these kidnappings runs deep. I try not to think of it, yet every day before falling asleep and when waking up, I think of them. What it must be like to be snatched from your house and taken to a vague, unfamiliar place. The youngest hostage is a baby who was captured at nine months old and had already turned ten months in captivity. There is a three year old girl who turns four tomorrow. All of us who watch kids grow up know how crucial these periods of time are in a child's life. These periods of time have been forever lost. On the other hand, there are senior citizens, pensioners at the age of eighty-five and upwards, who are either Holocaust survivors or who remember the end of the Second World War, who have been kidnapped. The idea of this recurring trauma is unimaginable.

This is the part in which I foresee some of the readers' responses and respond to them. Ah, you may think. But Israel is attacking many, many women, children and elderly people in Gaza. And has done so for years. The *New York Times* ran a piece in which it described Gaza as a cemetery for children. Why don't you speak up about this? you wonder, why this obsession with the Israeli hostages when the loss of life in Gaza is so much larger and more acute? My reply to this is manifold in its registers. First, we do speak of this, often. Many of us. We feel the pain and anger at this being done in our names, and condemn it where we can and when we can. But two wrongs don't make a right. And being silent about hostages being taken from their beds on a Saturday morning won't reduce the death toll in Gaza. If anything it will make Israelis feel more vulnerable and more under attack.

The more profound answer, though, is that there's something dehumanising and detached in playing this condemnation game with us, Israelis and Palestinians. In the same way I have resented the pressure to see condemnations of events of the 7th from Palestinian friends.

We know many of the hostages. Or the hostages' families. Or those who are supporting the families. Israel is a country of seven million people. 249 people are assumed to be held hostage. Many of them come from my circles: liberal, middle class, left-leaning. There's something deeply dehumanising in demanding we withdraw from our networks, from our families and friends, and take what *you*, the world, take to be the objectively correct position. These are my people and I care about them first. Wanting to save my family, my family's friends, my relatives' classmates doesn't mean I don't care about others' pain.

This moment in time, and especially the campaign to save the hostages (there is no doubt this hostage deal, as imperfect as it is, is a result of immense public pressure; people attending public events despite missile bombardments, marching to the Knesset in the rain, doing sit–ins and other forms of protest locally and internationally) is truly singular. This will continue until all hostages are safely back. Today I am going to a public installation at Israel's biggest dance venue (equivalent to Sadlers Wells in London or the Joyce in NYC) where a few choreographers have created a protest installation demanding the hostages to return home. All of them to return home. The executive director of said centre, whose daughter I taught ballet when she was twelve (have I mentioned we're a small country?) stood with me in the very first "free them all" rally and we escaped together to a bomb shelter when an alarm caught us outdoors.

It is hard to describe the tension in the air. We are all holding our breath in so many ways. We do not know who will be released and in what state they'll be. We don't know what this means for the other hostages: are they alive, or dead? Will their families get to see them? I cannot imagine what it's like for the families of the hostages. It's like a really cruel roulette. So today I am glad to have my dance community to pass the time with (before going to a dance class then attending a thanksgiving dinner to which I was very graciously and generously invited by another dancer friend). Have I said, thank god for dance?

Since the beginning of the war I've been listening to much more music in Hebrew. Retreating into my community and my networks while trying to preserve them, sustain them, give them strength and draw strength from them means it is easiest for me to feel in the language in which I was raised here; the language in which I completed my high school studies and my first two degrees, the language in which I read books first and wrote my first essays in high school. I've noticed that many songs I like are actually poems used by some of my favourite singers. For the past few weeks I've been listening to this song on repeat; there's a beautiful sung version by Israeli singer Yehudit Ravitz, but the lyrics are by poet Leah Goldberg (who used to live on my mother's street, have I mentioned this is a small country?). I've now seen this poem circulated widely on my Israeli social media networks as it's incredibly poignant for today. These days, until the hostages are back, and we know more about the ones left behind, are for this tense anticipation, to sustain my communities and my networks, the families of hostages waiting for their return and everyone supporting them. Waiting is so very hard.

## When one is attacked as a Jew(ess): reading Arendt after the 7th October

In August, I went to Aberdeen to speak at an Arendt conference. I had been away from academia for nearly two years and was flattered to get an insistent invitation. What's more, the occasion, marking fifty years since Arendt gave the Gifford Lectures that became her *The Life of the Mind*, one of my favourite books that I had been re-reading, for myself, before going to work (which at that point was advocating for freedom of movement in Gaza) was too compelling to refuse. I was invited to speak about Arendt and dance, something I had written about in my first and third books, though Arendt provided a helpful vista for my Rosa Luxemburg biography too; I had found her account of Luxemburg as pariah compelling.

The conference was very thoughtfully put together and from the beginning I found the conversations amicable and generative. This is not always the case in academic conferences, let alone those in which 'specialists' who work on one intellectual personality meet and contrast their reading of that personality. From the beginning, though, I found an undertone that was easily discernible. One of the first speakers referred to a panel on 'problematic Arendt' and said 'Is there any other Arendt?' to roars of laughter. Two keynote lectures out of a three–day conference were by scholars of African–American studies who had written on the race question in Arendt, one that she had got, pretty consensually now, wrong. It felt like a bizarre scheduling move, to organise a conference honouring someone, and then spend two evenings on their errors. I wonder if a male philosopher would have had the same treatment.

I love reading Arendt and have done so for the last twenty years of my life. In fact, reading *The Human Condition* as an undergraduate was the thing that got me hooked on political theory. She is also close to my heart for other reasons: when I did my Masters, I used her *Human Condition* (Arendtians: the purple edition with her face on it) while staying over at my grandmother, who once said to me casually: "Why are you reading this? She was never nice to me."

My grandmother hailed from Königsberg (now Kaliningrad), and I discovered that day was several years younger than Arendt at school, and friends with her cousin Liesel Aron. Arendt was already in Heidelberg then, my grandmother told me, and was snobbish to young girls who didn't understand philosophy.

My grandmother never finished high school. She came to Israel at around fourteen and went to work straight away. She had no idea that Arendt had become, well, Arendt.

I was very close to my grandmother. In fact, I chose my current flat in Tel Aviv as it's several blocks from my grandmother's house. During the summer I go to swim in the sea, something she did all her life, well into her nineties. My grandmother was an open, cheerful and generous woman. She rarely talked about her childhood in Germany and the whole world her family lost there. I knew we had, like many, lost relatives in the Holocaust, but also that my grandmother and her close family were exceptionally lucky and had fled early on.

So, for me, getting to know Arendt was also getting to know the culture from which I came. Arendt herself reminded me often of my grandmother: always well put together, pearls intact, hair neatly done, elegant. These were women who escaped a world that no longer exists.

So, whereas I have not much to say theoretically to the critique of Arendt and racism in America, I had this strong feeling in my gut, there was something she knew that they didn't. She had fled something no one really knew, even those with experiences of racism and oppression of other sorts.

One of the most helpful essays for me since the 7th was Ofri Ilany's essays in which he quotes her talking about knowing or not knowing what had happened in the camps, and/or refusing to engage in that. The correlation to the events of the 7th is easy to draw: so many had refused to believe what occurred that day, and still accuse Israel of exaggerating or even inventing those events in order to justify its attack on Gaza.

Straight after the attacks I went back to reading *The Origins of Totalitarianism*. I don't know why, I was just drawn back to this text, which grounded for me many questions circling in my mind: about the 7th October and about Israel's attacks in Gaza, both. Arendt's reading of human rights: as dependent on the nation–state thus excluding the most vulnerable, those without citizenship, felt especially timely.

But more and more I found myself drawn back to her biographical writings. In terms of her engagement with Israel, Arendt's critique, including her book on the Eichmann trial, as well as some critiques she makes in *The Jewish Writings*, still ring true to me. She was one of several intellectuals including Gershom

Scholem who supported Brith Shalom, an organisation that called for Israeli–Palestinian coexistence in a kind of one–state solution. Her ideas were well before their time, and in many ways, very accurate. I find her ideas helpful to understand Israel's attack on Gaza as well as its deepening regime of occupation and apartheid.

But there was one sentence that particularly circled in my mind since the 7th. When reminiscing about her childhood she said that her mother taught her how to respond to anti-Semitism: when one is attacked as a Jew, one must defend oneself as a Jew. Not as a German, not as a world citizen, not as an upholder of the Rights of Man.

I found this sentence rushing through my head also with regard to something I had been working really hard to repress and chase away from my brain: sexual violence used against Israeli women in the 7th October attacks. There is ample evidence and documentation that as part of their attacks on Israelis living in the south of Israel, Hamas terrorists raped and used sexual violence as a weapon of war. I find my breathing getting heavy as I write this. The response to these pieces of evidence internationally has been faint, which led Israeli feminists to launch a campaign called "#MeToo unless you're a Jew".

I want to start by saying that I hate this campaign. I hate it so much. Much like Arendt, I find Israel's use of its victim position abhorrent. Israel is not the weak and meek country it presents itself to the world, and as Arendt discussed eloquently in the 1960s, it has often played this card to efface its own wrongs. It is wrongdoer rather than victim. I think in many of the cases in which Israel has been made a pariah state this has been justified, as a country upholding the longest occupation in modern times.

But there is no way, in any political, legal or ethical configuration, that one can find justification for use of rape as a weapon of war.

Like many women, this is not a theoretical issue for me. Like many women, this current trauma builds on other experiences I have lived through. I am, as I had written here before, grateful to have a strong network around me of women advocating feminist human rights and international law. I turned to them over the past few weeks and found we were all stuck with this, this horrible thing that we couldn't process.

The combination of misogyny and racism is toxic. We know that well from all anti-racist struggles. But, as Arendt knew well, anti-Semitism has its own unique strands of racism. There are ways in which intellectual, well-spoken, "correct on everything else" people can still be deeply anti-Semitic. Arendt's writing on anti-Semitism on the left has been especially helpful to me over the past weeks. The idea that if one is good on x, y and z one understands a and b correctly is a fantasy, something some of us who want to be "right about everything" had created for themselves.

But like Arendt, I have been attacked as a Jew, and I am finding it hard to cope with thinking of these women who had been attacked as Jewesses.

This national trauma we're living through is still too big to put into words, or to process effectively. One of my favourite responses to "from the river to the sea" was "from the river to the sea we all need therapy". That is very precise.

I don't quite know what it means to me to defend myself as a Jewess. I know personally for me it had meant going back to

Arendt, Zigmunt Bauman, Simone Weil, Etty Hillesum, Jacques Derrida, Emmanuel Levinas, as well as contemporary Israeli writers such as David Grossman (of course), Ofri Ilany, Michal Ben Naftali, Amos Oz, Meir Shalev, Ronit Matalon, Leah Goldberg, Yonah Wallach and others. Having the books written by people thinking in my mother tongue and from my culture is my first line of defence (I'm also thinking of Arendt's quote: "What remains? The mother tongue remains." which feels really poignant right now). I know it's going back into my community and reaching to my solidarity networks. Those who understand and know.

But I also know that I don't know. I don't know how to defend myself as a Jewess

When I fall asleep I pray that if there is a recurrence of the 7th October attack, a scenario we're all dreading, they'll kill me on the spot. No kidnapping, no rape. That is my only wish. That is at the moment my defence.

An hour and a half left till the first hostages are released. I shall return to Arendt and hope for better times, a peaceful Shabbat, a Shabbat of peace.

25.11.2023

## Hanging between life and death

Today is the second day of the ceasefire. It is warm again, after having a bit of rain earlier in the week. The evenings are getting chillier though, signifying that time had indeed passed over the last fifty days that also feel frozen.

Yesterday afternoon was one of the most extraordinary experiences of my life. I wish with all my might that no one has to live through this. I really appreciate people who say to me "I can't imagine what it's like". The truth is *we* can't imagine what it's like, and we're living it. I don't have a name for "it" yet, but I know it is my reality.

The ceasefire deal was deferred from Thursday to Friday, then the hostage exchange postponed to the evening. That was very worrying. A friend I saw on Thursday said to me she's afraid the hostage exchange will be bodies actually sent back. I had considered that and pushing the exchange to Friday evening made it more of a possibility, as it was due to take place after Shabbat had gone in.

In Israel we say when something is very quiet "it's like Yom Kippur", indicating that no cars are driving on the street. Yesterday was beyond Yom Kippur, as usually kids ride their bikes on the roads during Yom Kippur, a secular tradition. The roads were empty. You could have heard a pin drop from 16:00—the time the hostages were due to pass into Egyptian hands. I met a friend from dance to help her with a funding application. It was also a good way to pass the time. We had both nervously looked at our phones, but as I was walking home through a quiet Tel Aviv nothing had come in yet. Then I started staring at the news.

Then the images came in. First, some grey-haired women sitting in Red Cross ambulances. I started sobbing then, and continued, not knowing whether it's tears of happiness: they were alive, and seemed OK, walking independently, or sorrow—what they must have gone through, what they must feel like at this moment. Then more footage was flowing. In addition to the first round of hostages released—thirteen yesterday, and this is due to be repeated every day of the ceasefire—also twelve foreign workers (mostly Thai but also one from the Philippines) were released. It is so bizarre and horrific to think of them held in Gaza without any connection to the war, the occupation, or anything really. I was so glad to see them.

Then a woman and a young girl walking. A family with a child. By now, we know all their names. We know their stories. The boy released, Ohad, had his birthday while in captivity, he turned nine. His friends said they're waiting for him to have a joint birthday celebration. How can people be so terrible and yet so wonderful? I ask myself every day of this horror.

Then, a list of names is released and confirmed. We get clearer images of those people released. We know they are safe. We try to think about what they lived through, but we can't. And the heart and brain wanders to those who are still there. Who may be released over the next few days of the ceasefire, or not. Somehow seeing them, older women, young children, walking escorted by the Red Cross made it all feel so visceral and real. These are people like us who were held in Gaza for seven weeks. And there are more. These are our family friends, friends, families… who went through something we cannot even imagine, and yet it is there, on our TV screens.

A video has been circulated on Israeli social media showing Sky News broadcaster Kay Burley rolling her eyes when hearing she has to hear about the hostages again. I realise also for the readers of this you may feel the same. Not again, the hostages. But for us, it's the first and most important thing. To save them means to save ourselves.

I went on a long run this morning, and felt a relief, also in my ballet class yesterday, that I didn't have to fear an alarm due to a missile bombardment. Never in my life have I felt so close to death, all the time. Running on the Tel Aviv promenade alongside the beach till Yaffa with many runners who could only talk about one thing: the hostages release and what next.

Death is everywhere. We feel it in our midst. It is lurking behind corners, unexpected yet always present. Israel doesn't release exact locations of missiles that have fallen so that Hamas doesn't get feedback on the accuracy of their launches and yet as time passes I hear from more and more friends of proximity of missiles falling near them, hearing a missile above their heads when they were caught outside during a missile bombardment alarm. This is our reality right now, and I honestly do not wish it to anyone.

But then there's Gaza. Like many, I am following the news from there with horror. I see the photos of what seem like mass graves, one near the other. The death toll exceeds anything a human being can fathom. It is very close to us. It is part of us. There is so much death everywhere.

The one thing I realised this period is that survival is a stronger impulse than I had considered. Before alarms go off I have an inner conversation with myself: maybe this time I'll let the alarm go and not run to the bomb shelter. I'm fed up with it all. Conversations with neighbours have exhausted themselves. And running up and down four floors is not fun. And yet every time an alarm goes off I bolt. I don't think. I am in survival mode.

It's very clear to me in Gaza there is nowhere to run. People must be pushed beyond survival mode, knowing their chances of saving themselves are very slim. I can't imagine what that is like. I am horrified it is being done in my name. I just want this all over.

Today, for the International Day of Eradicating Violence Against Women, I am going to a meeting of Palestinian and Jewish women about the war. And then, in the evening, a rally for the families of the hostages. I cannot imagine what it might be like to experience yesterday if you have a loved one in Gaza. All I can do is give my solidarity to all those who are hanging between life and death. And keep up the hope for better days. After the war.

30.11.2023

## How the politics of self-care and self-medication collapse into the politics of the virtuous victim or: it's not about you

With time, I realise that the time in which I originally started to write this blog: the beginning of the COVID pandemic, and our current moment here in Israel–Palestine aren't that distinct, especially when it comes to international responses. There were several issues that bothered me then and I find bother me now, or rather several tendencies I find collapsing into different iterations that have similar sources. I'll start with a flashback.

In the West, broadly defined, especially the English-speaking West ie. the US and the UK, I had noticed a tendency to both self-diagnose with a whole lot of issues, mostly related to the broadly construed field of mental health, and gain responses that equally were focused on individual treatment that assumes drawing away from society. This sounds pompous but is simple. With time, I noticed many people around me stopped having bad days or feeling upset. Everyone was struggling with depression or anxiety. I'm not talking, of course, of people who are diagnosed by medical professionals but the laymen who kept saying to the world: leave me alone, I am suffering, and this is serious suffering. To be clear and to be fair, in my books it's perfectly OK to say (pardon my language): fuck off, I've had a bad day, especially when one is living amidst a global pandemic, say, or a war, yet this now feels impossible. We all have to be "suffering" from something and for it to be medicalised. Appropriately, at the time, I had written here about my aversion to what I will call "the politics of self-care". This means in response to being overwhelmed with the total and utter collapse of the welfare state, the fact that our collective couldn't hold us at a moment of great crisis, and that we felt alone and marginalised, we retreated into the self even more, supplemented by many capitalist goodies, such as bubble baths and facial masks (sorry for the gendered nature of the examples, these were the ones most prevalent). There was little or no dissent and no collective response. The response was to retreat into the self and to consume more, without regarding capitalism's role in said failures of the collectives.

Fast forward three years, and yet another global crisis is upon us. Once again I see people around me collapse into similar discourses. To be clear: I'm not so much talking about Israelis and Palestinians as we don't have much time or possibility to practice all the above, though emotional eating has certainly grown in our areas and everyone is smoking and drinking more.

I'm talking more of international discourse around Israel/Palestine and how it's framed. With time that passes the grave disagreements become more and more about the perception of the individual posting, their positioning to the issues at hand, and especially how much suffering they can perform.

The articulation of these issues is different to the ones I described above during COVID, but the location and consequence is the same: the problems start and end with the self, rather than thinking collectively and analysing power structures.

I was helpfully reminded to return to the writing of Anat Matar, one of my all time favourite leftist writers here who critiqued the idea of the virtuous victim. The victim who is so absolute they can do no wrong, and are vindicated by the fact that they are victims, to which the relationship is one of compassion or even pity rather than solidarity. Now, this leads to a very curious race to the bottom, not that different when one thinks about it than the over-medicalisation of suffering. It is only the most oppressed, the most depressed, that we must listen to. And they then gain power over all morality. Suffering becomes fetishised and aspired towards.

When it comes to Israel–Palestine it is very clear there are people who have become victims of violence something between ethnic cleansing and genocide. These are the 2.2 million civilians in Gaza. It is clear we must listen to them and their witness. But what about everyone else? If you are a "victim" of racism, if you suffered some kind of oppression, does this give you some kind of upper hand in an argument? Are all oppressions the same? I argued here earlier that anti-Semitism is distinct from other sorts of racism. I feel very uneasy commenting on or critiquing forms of racism I haven't experienced. So how come everyone who has experienced racism in any form can comment on anti-Semitism and should be considered an authority? Can victims (I use the term with reference to the virtuous victim configuration) of anti-Black racism understand the racism that people of Gaza experience better? And should they be treated as authorities?

First and foremost, it's clear we should listen to people's narratives of their own experience. But second, we should be cautious of fetishizing suffering as well as making available only individual routes for emancipation. Because if you should only listen to *me* because of the specific sets of circumstances that made *me* oppressed, it is hard for me to organise with people who are not like me, find mutual enemies and common causes. The Palestinian marches were impressive for the wide audiences they brought out. But when looking, and especially discussing, the issues with individuals in and in response to social media, it very often returned to *me*. Why aren't you responding to *my* argument? What about *my* perspective?

And this is where the subheading of this essay comes into play. It is not about you. If you are an organiser you care about bringing people out to an action, not about how they perceive you. If you care about your image or return from the matter at hand into your own issues, take a look at what motivated you for action in the first place.

One of the many problems of this virtuous victim discourse is that it glosses over power imbalances. It glosses over the so-called victim mobilising their voice towards those with whom they are meant to be in solidarity. It very often takes matters in isolation and without context. Thinking about this also clarified to me why I despised the discourse Israeli women generated about sexual violence on the 7th October so much: the campaigns and framing tried to position them as the absolute victim. But, like everything in life, no one is that. You can be a victim and an oppressor at the same time: most of us are, and none of us are completely virtuous. Israel is a strong country with a strong army, supported by other countries whose strong armies sent it ammunition several days after the attacks. It became victim to a terrorist assault in a complex context, but this puts it in line much more with the US post-9/11, UK after the July bombings, and Paris following various terrorist attacks, rather than people in Gaza.

If we were to try and find solutions to structural issues, power imbalances and respond to inequalities, the response will have to be collective and decentralise the self. If we really want to find a way to defend the rights of the people of Gaza, it has to be about *them*, not your experience or your suffering or insult or wanting to get traction on your social media.

And, to end on a lighter note, whereas everyone here is high on various kinds of medication (self-medication mostly), weed, booze, and everything else that helps us survive, I'm pleased to say that here it's still an acceptable answer to say "things are shit because there's an ongoing war" and we haven't all fallen into DSM diagnosis. I think being honest about how bad things are and what might be their causes: pandemic and war will help us also find a way to mobilise collectively and not think of ourselves as suffering all the time. It's also a much nicer way to live life. Honestly.

# DECEMBER

A Christmas wish from around the corner
from a little town of Bethlehem

## A birthday wish

It's my birthday today.

The two people I know personally got their family members back, so that's one wish granted. I did not know what to say to them: congratulations on your loved one returning from enemy captivity? Not quite the Hallmark card, but a huge sense of relief. I sent them a heart emoji as what can one say?

There are still quite a few hostages left behind.

Today the ceasefire expires. There was a shooting attack in Jerusalem yesterday that killed four and injured seven people. Hamas claimed responsibility.

This annihilated any hope I had that the ceasefire would just be naturally extended.

I have only one wish this birthday, for this awful war to end, and for the end of it to bring some kind of viable political solution that allows all, Palestinians and Israelis from the river to the sea, to live peacefully and without fear.

I have to keep hoping I'll get my birthday wish.

It's weird to receive all sorts of "happy birthday" messages as no one is happy. I went out with a good friend yesterday who brought me cake and champagne. We spoke for two hours, only about the war.

No one is in any kind of celebratory mood. I'll go to ballet class, I've always danced on my birthday, then a Zoom meeting of a human rights organisation I'm involved with, then will go and stay with my mother, for a sense of togetherness.

Things are so unclear and so heavy. I honestly just want this to end.

At least Henry Kissinger died and there's one fewer war criminal in the world.


05.12.2023

In memory of Fatmeh Salem

Yesterday we got the sad news that Fatmeh Salem had died. The inimitable matriarch of the Salem family of Sheikh Jarrah, which has been fighting to stay in its home for decades, died without seeing any resolution to her struggle, without knowing that her family will have a house to live in.

Whereas the death toll in Gaza continues to climb in incomprehensible numbers, Fateh's death somehow hit me hard. I got involved in the struggle against evictions in Sheikh Jarrah and Silwan shortly after returning to Israel–Palestine in 2021. These two areas in East Jerusalem, Palestinian communities with rich history, are fighting a hard legal battle against settler associations which are trying to displace them through old and expired property claims, arguing that indeed these are Jewish regions of Jerusalem. None of the settlers who are trying to expel Palestinians from East Jerusalem have any direct connections to these areas. One particularly interesting legal case is that of Michael ben Yair, former Israeli Attorney General, one of the only people who can prove that his family had some ownership in this area (in his case, Silwan). He publicly renounces it and yet settlers claim they have the right to *his* home by virtue of Jewish association.

The struggle against evictions in East Jerusalem was one of my first lessons in how Jewish supremacy is enacted through the courts, which often validate the settlers' claims, and give a rubber stamp to violent acts of displacement. I had also encountered this first hand, working with some of the lawyers representing those families, what it's like trying to be a voice against a system that doesn't want to hear you.

Back to Fatmeh Salem. When I was the Director of Peace Now, I got a call saying that there was a solidarity visit of the Meretz Party MKs to the Salem family. I decided to join. Two MKs I worked closely with, Gaby Lasky (one of the most inspirational human rights lawyers here), and Mossi Raz (who was Director of Peace Now when I was a child in the movement and is truly one of the most irrepressible campaigners I had ever met) were greeted like royalty. Other MKs were pleasantly hosted. Fatmeh sat in the centre of the room, and we all came and shook her hand. We were waiting for yet another verdict on her house. Suddenly, news came through; the verdict had been postponed, by a few months. We went outside. An impromptu party was organised in Sheikh Jarrah. There was dancing and merriment. The community was celebrating not being evicted for a few more months. Fatmeh was lifted on a chair. I remember feeling both vicarious joy, which was overflowing then, and misery. How can one celebrate not being illegally and immorally being evicted from your family home?

Whenever I went to protests in Sheikh Jarrah, Fatmeh was there. She spoke often in Israeli events, rare for the Palestinian community in Sheikh Jarrah.

I feel this is an important moment to reflect on why or why not to work with Israelis in these kinds of struggles. Many Palestinians fighting displacement and ethnic cleansing either refuse or have lost hope in the Israeli judicial system. They know it is a façade of justice re-enacting settler interests, be it in the South Hebron Hills, East Jerusalem, or elsewhere. Some reluctantly go to the courts, represented by either Palestinians or Israelis, yet don't work politically with Israelis. Some do go to the courts and work with Israelis.

I understand all choices and have never resented any Palestinian comrade who did not want to work with me. Indeed, there are some complaints against certain associations that whitewash the occupation and apartheid, that give a façade of "coexistence" and working together whereas indeed these associations simply re-enact power imbalances while giving the Israelis the feel-good element of "we have a Palestinian friend". I understand the resentment towards those associations and have felt angry myself when I was pushed to be the face of them. However, it is clear that nothing here will move without some kind of dialogue, even if not collaboration or presenting a façade of something that doesn't exist, between Palestinians and Israelis on the ground. Very often these collaborations are behind the scenes; indeed, a good test to all those working towards such collaborations is: do you feel the need for them to be visible so that you receive kudos, or are you happy for your voice to be used without you collecting any gain? But even those which include, at times, safeguarding Palestinian communities against settler violence, especially in the Masafer Yatta region, are not easy and can get resistance from all sides.

So, I always felt Fatmeh Salem's generosity and humanity was undeserved by us. Whenever she came to me and shook my hand, I felt deeply ashamed, and that I did not deserve that treatment. What was I doing? I was failing in holding my state to account to secure her home. Yet, that always also gave me hope, that someone can be as generous as that, as larger than life as that, to see something beyond the state, the person who is there in front of you, fighting with you, and to be able to shake their hands. I wish we all had half of Fatmeh Salem's moral courage and humanity. The world would be a better place.

Rest in power, Fatmeh Salem. We have failed you, as a community of resistance. But we will keep fighting for justice and for your family to finally find peace in their home.

07.12.2023

## Gaga dance class for human rights in the middle of a war

Yesterday I attended a donation class taught by Ohad Naharin, House Choreographer of the Batsheva Dance Company, by far the most significant dance company in Israel. I have been taking Gaga classes for about six years. My introduction to Gaga wasn't straightforward. I first took a class here and didn't enjoy it, I think around eight years ago. When I lived in NYC Gaga was all the rage and I realised I didn't want to pay huge NYC class fees for something invented on my doorstep. I took a few classes when I went back home for a vacation and have been hooked ever since.

I'll write later about what Gaga means to me, but first I wanted to say a few things about why it was significant for me to take class yesterday.

Over the past few months there has been a culture war declared, mainly via Instagram, on Batsheva (and Martha Graham, the company's first choreographer), Ohad and Gaga as enabling and legitimising Israeli settler colonialism and connecting it to American settler colonialism. The war started with a pithy video posted in which in a lecture-style delivery a young woman (no last name, affiliation, goes by the name of Leila) "explains" these issues. My stomach turned when I first saw the video (and then again, when a well-meaning but completely politically ignorant dance friend sent it to me with "I thought you'd like to see this"—I haven't spoken to her since). I don't want to spend too much time on this video, not least because my friend, a brilliant dance writer and one of my favourite Gaga teachers Deborah Friedes Galili wrote a response which provides a short and precise rebuttal to the misinformation in the video. If you have seen the video, I strongly encourage you to read this response, easily found online at danceinisrael.com, under 'In Defence of Responsible Dance Research: a wartime response'.

I will say in my own voice a few things about the to and fro that continued. Personally, I have no objection to Boycott, Divestment, Sanctions (BDS) as a non-violent resistance to Israeli occupation and apartheid, and as a way to resist whitewashing of occupation through culture. I have spoken about this publicly and think the legal attacks against BDS are very dangerous. I can also very well understand why Naharin and Batsheva have become a symbol for BDS, not least because the success of the company and Gaga made him, alongside David Grossman, one of the most famous Israeli cultural exports. But I do have a few objections to the way this culture war has been declared, and some reservations about its efficacy, which is why I'm writing this post. Posting a more-or-less anonymous video in which you spread false information and provide hyperbolic arguments by way of performing "explainers" is dangerous. We are in a post-truth era but there are facts, and they do matter. Anyway, enough about that.

Since returning to Israel I've been taking mainly a mix of ballet and Gaga classes. I'm not a Gaga scholar so will write more from my own point of view rather than anything formal or choreography-oriented. Gaga is a movement research practice invented by Naharin and practised daily by his dancers at Batsheva. It is a different way of understanding space and movement within it than any other movement system, and also the possibilities within ones body. The class is taught when the teacher stands in the centre of the class, everyone is around her/him in a circle, no mirrors are involved. Dancers move according to imaginative instructions: imagine you're moving through water, imagine you're a bodybuilder and the thickness of your muscles comes through your movement... and so on. The research also tries to mobilise various parts of the body which are usually dead, including in other dance techniques. Gaga has made me aware of details of my body and how I move in space in a way I had never felt before. There's something about thinking of the body differently that makes you move differently. One of the main reasons I love Gaga is that as a person with a short attention span, the need to listen to constant instructions makes me aware and alert and constantly engaged, and my body moves like in no other technique. No class is the same and Gaga is a good antidote to the very structured form of ballet. Gaga breathes life into my spine and makes it move like nothing else I've ever practised in my life.

Naharin is a significant figure here. He has been outspoken on many issues including signing statements against forcible transfer of Palestinians in the South Hebron Hills, for example, and many other such solidarity statements. He has taught for a long time this donation class to support Association of Civil Rights in Israel, the equivalent of the American Civil Liberties Union or Liberty in the UK. In the invitation to the class there was a short paragraph about why ACRI is so significant, especially at this moment. Which is why the Instagram campaign making him the face of the occupation feels so misguided and frankly, ridiculous. There is enough to critique Batsheva and Ohad but this is not one of those ways.

Anyway, beyond the political agenda, I do want to write about the significance of Ohad and Batsheva for me, personally. I grew up in the 90s seeing his work evolve. His work was the thing that got me hooked on dance and understood its endless possibilities. Throughout the years the company was home to some of my favourite dancers to watch (who are now Gaga teachers and with whom I share a studio, a boon in its own right). Batsheva dancers move like nothing you've seen before. With all critique of Gaga, it works. The suppleness of movement and the deconstruction of the body is truly unique to Ohad's work with the company. He is, without doubt, one of the few truly significant living choreographers of our time, whose legacy has changed the way we see dance. No wonder Gaga is so popular around the world.

Last time I went to the American Dance Festival in Durham, as a resident scholar, there were waiting lists to enrol in Gaga class (no such thing for Graham, alas; poor Martha!).

Gaga is taught in Batsheva's own building, and yesterday the class took place in the studio in which the company rehearses. It feels really special to be at the heart of where creativity comes from, where the work is constructed (today I'm going to see the company perform *Momo*, Naharin's latest work). In the true manner of Israeliness, everything is open and, a Gaga term used a lot, available. You have to be available to movement. And things are open to many people around Gaga. Gaga can be taught for dancers but also—and these are the classes I'm taking—to people, where no previous experience is required and honestly the widest variety of people come to move together. I would say a majority of the class are people who would never go to any other class and are truly not dancers. But they want to move and are granted the space solely by Gaga.

Yesterday I had a terrible day of multiple deadlines and minor anxieties. I was contemplating whether to go to class. I did something uncharacteristic for myself and pushed myself to the inner circle around Ohad and two beautiful company dancers. I danced for an hour opposite them. It was magic. Ohad is seventy and moves so beautifully, it was inspiring to feed off his energy and think about what it means for me and my body at this moment. There were hundreds of people who paid a handsome sum for charity.

At the end of the class Ohad gave a speech about ACRI and said something that really stayed with me. He spoke about how our contract with the state is broken right now, but our responsibilities to each other by virtue of being human remain and are more important than ever. I must confess that made me tear up. It was really important at this moment.

The more time passes in this war the more I understand the biggest challenge is to stay human and humane. To be open and available for others. It felt very special to share in Ohad's generous spirit at this moment and for human rights. It was an evening that will carry me for a long time.

08.12.2023

## The passing of time during a war

Yesterday marked two months since the beginning of the war, and the first candle of Hanukkah. The war started on the last day of Sukkot. I have never felt less festive on Hanukkah, a holiday I always loved. I just got my period for the third time this war. These are the external markers showing us something has changed on the calendar since 7th October. To me it feels like time has stood still. I almost feel angry when I have to change the calendar pages.

Yesterday it was announced that one of Israel's politicians lost his son in the attacks on Gaza. Gadi Eisenkot, who had himself been Chief of Staff, now sits in the war cabinet. I have just heard him deliver a eulogy, with a broken voice, at his son's grave.

The death count in Gaza has reached 17,000 at least. This makes no sense to me.

Mentally, it feels like time has stopped completely on the 7th. All other markers of time feel tangential. As I wrote here, it was my birthday this time last week. I had never felt less celebratory, not least because it seemed unreal enough time had lapsed for my birthday to actually arrive.

The feeling is that we're trapped in several time spans simultaneously. There is the international calendar that takes no notice of our little corner in the Middle East. The disparity between that and our timeline was first felt on Halloween. Everyone who had been posting online about Gaza or Israel suddenly was posting their cute Halloween costumes/kids in Halloween costumes. I felt more than a pang of bitterness; for us, disengaging the timeline of this horrid war is not an option. Then, that feeling of parallel times intensified with Thanksgiving. Once again I felt both some relief going online wasn't going to send me into strange rabbit holes, but also the fact that the timeline in which I was living was now completely out of vision for many people around me.

Then, there is, as I write, our timeline here. National days of mourning, markers. The ceasefire, which sent us back into a time we once had, a time of possibility. Neither here nor there. A hiatus. Now, a Jewish holiday. I love Hanukkah. Any holiday that brings light in the winter (not that we have here any sense of winter) is always cherished. This year it feels like no one around me wants to celebrate anything. The Menorahs in Tel Aviv are attracting far less people for public candle lighting and doughnuts than usual. The city feels odd. 300,000 people are still on reserve duty. Throughout the country it is noticeable there are far less young men around. And at times, especially on weekends, tired young men in uniforms with guns walk around. No one wants to ask them anything about what they saw and what they had done.

I cannot imagine what their timeline will feel like, if it has any logic to it at all. My friends on reserve duty text when they can, and then have tired conversations on breaks. I don't know what to ask them either.

Going back to the outside world, I am very aware that Christmas fever is taking over everywhere. It feels even more bizarre as I have heard now, from different Christian Palestinian friends, that there is an overarching decision not to mark Christmas here this year, in Palestine; to be precise, in Nazareth, in Bethlehem. The irony of connecting this to the Christian narrative on a whole is not lost. The world cares about Gaza/Israel/Palestine until the world celebrates a holiday that actually happened here according to its narrative.

When I lived in the UK I always found it humorous to hear these Israeli–Palestinian towns uttered in the most British accents in Christmas carols, whereas they were in fact around the corner from me.

Many analyses I've read, and some I've been kindling myself, see these next few weeks as the last window of opportunity to demand a ceasefire and end this war. If Western states pressure Israel to enter negotiations it will have to stop its fighting. Once we're entering late December/January, public offices are far less staffed, then we're entering the winter months. People's thoughts will be elsewhere. And who knows what else will happen till then to attract attention and become the most important thing.

And so, I've been feeling for a while, like I've been constantly falling into an anxious limbo. Waiting for something to change, for a stop to all this. Without any knowledge of how time can look differently. A time with no anxiety. Without running to shelters as I did, just an hour ago, when a heavy missile bombardment hit Tel Aviv.

For now, it feels almost offensive that time passes. I don't want any holidays or festivities or celebrations until there's an ease in the air. Then time can start, properly, and perhaps a different time, one marked with hope as its horizon, one which has an open, generous rhythm, that looks into the future with open eyes.

09.12.2023

## How I learnt to love philosophy through realising I'm an atheist Jewess in Israel

Yesterday, like most Fridays over the past weeks, I went to my favourite independent bookstore in Neve Tzedek, Sipur Pashut. Over the years, I made friends and interlocutors through this store, brilliant women who brought new ideas, conversations and thoughts into my life. I would say in addition to dance, reading and thinking has been my mainstay over this war. I got myself a birthday gift, a few books I had coveted including a collection of essays by Derrida and Walter Benjamin.

I was really tired yesterday evening. After the first alarm I had written about (which brought damage to a Tel Aviv neighbourhood not far from me) there was a second alarm three hours later. I was jumpy throughout the evening, and as I went to sleep, I realised I was just waiting for the third alarm, and fourth, and so on.

Meanwhile, horrific stories of the abducted are coming out, making bringing back the hostages more and more urgent. I had struggled to conjure energy to light candles, but today I'll go to a candle lighting with the families of the hostages, which feels like the most meaningful thing to do this Hanukkah.

Anyway, despite a hard and long week I found myself compelled to read and annotate my new book. I started taking notes on Derrida. Derrida has been a blind spot for me for years; I had written most of my DPhil thesis based on Rancière, had taught Foucault and engaged with him quite a lot, and Levinas has been a constant inspiration for me since my graduate days. I had read some Derrida here and there, but never properly, and it felt like a huge black hole I didn't enter. Before the war I picked up an interview of one of my favourite Israeli authors, Michal Ben-Naftali with Derrida about philosophy after Auschwitz. Michal Ben Naftali was Derrida's student and interlocutor. This gained a different meaning, of course, during the war and devastation incurred by us and to us. And so, I felt this was, perhaps, a good moment to try and read more Derrida.

Over the past few weeks, I had thought about how much I love philosophy, essays, reading and of course writing, though writing is not a "love" for me as much as a necessity, what I do in order to think more clearly. And I had thought of some moments in my life that opened that window for me.

I think my favourite high school teacher deserves a more extensive tribute. I was, unsurprisingly to many of you, a nerd in high school. I liked books and studying was easy for me, especially the humanities. In my tenth grade we had a new teacher. Tal was young, twenty-seven when she started teaching us. She came from a Yemenite household and spoke openly and freely of her family's experience coming to Israel, the racism they had encountered, and the racism she still encounters. She was beautiful and charming, and I was completely smitten with her. She had the habit of writing us each personal notes in significant events: each of us got a birthday greeting, and we got notes for Rosh Hashana. She was brilliant and challenged me like no one I had met before. She taught Sociology, which I of course then decided to take as an extra subject (and with her I first read the *Communist Manifesto*), and she also taught Bible studies. In Israeli Jewish education Bible studies are a big deal. You start them in primary school, and they go on throughout your studies, with a final compulsory exam. I came from a totally secular household that celebrated Jewish high holidays culturally, with a Christian family who celebrated Christmas, also culturally. But I found out, early on, that I didn't dislike the Bible. I enjoyed reading it. The stories were good! A whole history of tales around some places I recognised from my own geography and some I didn't, but more on that later. Tal was an extraordinary teacher in both her subjects. She taught through asking questions and opening up conversations with us. She took us, her students, very seriously. Something I had hoped to embody when I was teaching myself, seeing your students as equals.

Around the age of thirteen-fourteen, right before I met Tal, I realised I was an atheist. I didn't believe in god. It's not that I didn't care about the history with/without him, I did. I just didn't think this was an essence that existed. I didn't dislike cultural rituals. I think each culture needs that, and especially Jewishness, which was for so many centuries hunted down and persecuted, needed something to unite around. Around that time I had joined Peace Now and became politically active. I had started asking questions about how Jewishness was abused and used to silence other religions and cultures, namely Muslim and Palestinian, but I was still and am still proud to be Jewish.

I was also very aware, especially later in life when living in the diaspora myself, that I am Israeli. As opposed to some readings that see Jews as always outsiders, bound to be in diaspora as minorities and perhaps out of their longstanding suffering can be some kind of moral leading lights to others, I think Jewishness and sovereignty are not antithetical. That whatever emerges of this complicated land I call home, it can be a home to Jews and Palestinians together, but that we don't have to forever seek to be the minorities and outsiders, just as long as we don't make others outsiders in the name of our religion. Anyway, back to my Bible studies. The years were the mid-late 1990s. The Oslo Accords brought a new spring of optimism to the region.

I had started to meet Palestinian youth of my age through Peace Now and realised how different we were, yet that they were part of this land as much as I was. In the tenth grade, just as I had started studying with Tal, I had won third place in a national essay writing competition marking Israel's fiftieth anniversary of independence from the British mandate. I had written something about the need to incorporate minorities into civic life in Israel. In hindsight, I didn't agree with myself then on some of the ways I had suggested, but the intent was there! I went with my mother and literature teacher to the prize ceremony in Jerusalem and gave a passionate speech in front of the Minister of Education about our moral responsibilities. The prize was four hundred NIS (about fifty pounds) in book vouchers. I was elated.

Anyway, back to Bible studies! One day, I came cautiously to

Tal, and told her that I was an atheist. She came from a religious home and was from the Masorti tradition so had respect for religion in a different way to me. I worshipped the ground she walked on and had spent time contemplating that difference between us. I came to her and told her I was an atheist, more of a dramatic coming out than anything related to sexuality, I think! She took it, as ever, really well. She said to me, OK. How about we read the Bible, together, if you take god out of the equation? If you treat god as another figure in the text, not *the* figure? Decades later, after encountering different readings of religion, I had realised what generosity and grace this must have demanded of her. And so, my journey with the Bible began anew. I started reading the Bible without god, or with god as an equal persona. Of course it changed the meaning of the text completely, and some elements of it worked less well than others. I had come to Tal after class (I mentioned I was a nerd!) and asked to sit with her, and we argued about certain elements that didn't work on these readings, or didn't make sense at all, and wondered together about chapters that were innately problematic. Derrida's *Aporia*, perhaps? But all in all, in hindsight, it was an early on deep dive into hermeneutics and philosophy without knowing it. When I started my academic studies philosophy came easy to me, and only years later I had realised where the practice came from. Perhaps it's not coincidental that many of the great philosophers of the twentieth century were Jewish: from Arendt though Levinas and Derrida to Butler.

Anyway, I owe a lot to Tal and those patient conversations, and think much of my passion for philosophy, for diving deep into textual problems and enjoying encountering texts from different perspectives is thanks to her. I ended up getting one of the highest marks on my Bible final exam and even attended extra lectures in Haifa University's Bible Studies department (I mentioned I was a nerd!). I was still on and off in touch with Tal. When I finished my DPhil I wrote to her and thanked her. She wrote back, "You were always a professor".

In hindsight I think, also, that these conversations also primed me to another mainstay of my life, sitting and discussing and arguing and disagreeing and agreeing with women I respect and love, as equals, about texts and ideas and crises and possibilities.

And with that, this Shabbat, third candle of Hanukkah, I shall return to Derrida.

11.12.2023

Discussed: Sometimes the night is a prayer for a different tomorrow, or how I managed to avoid becoming a self-hating Jewess

Yesterday I returned from our weekly editorial meeting and heard an uncannily familiar voice on my street in central Tel Aviv. It was beloved singer-songwriter Yoni Rechter, singing an assortment of his most popular songs in a show for all the family for Hanukkah not far from where I live. I smiled to myself, opened the window, and sang along when I was working. I was also swept by a memory; on the day of my DPhil viva I went running in Oxford's picturesque Port Meadow and listened to some of his songs, especially one that encourages the listener to be brave and proud. It helped. My life in Oxford generally feels like a different life to me now, but this coincidence of literally stumbling on one of my favourite songs on my doorstep after seeking it so far away made me happier considering everything. Tel Aviv Municipality is organising various events for the community, with the mood very subdued, many families torn with some still in reserve duty, and kids away from school, hence the performance.

That afternoon I had contemplated the fact that throughout my life I had many diverse and sometimes contradictory cultural passions and managed to harbour them alongside each other. I find various forms of culture nurturing and eye-opening, and being raised in a bilingual household that presented to me always two cultures without the need to put them in hierarchies made me always suspicious of the need to rank and order culture.

Perhaps in continuation to the last post I wrote here, I also remembered a few days ago that one of my earliest philosophical passions was Heidegger. Notoriously difficult to read, I decided to write a seminar about him in my Masters. Perhaps it was because I was told he was difficult, but I found him fascinating. My seminar compared and contrasted similar writing on language and nothingness of Heidegger and the Israeli national poet, Haim Nachman Bialik, in their respective historical context. Years later, when I was an academic, I ran into my supervisor who remembered that seminar. When I was writing my PhD I returned to that reading as I took a course in editing historical texts and contextualising them, and went deeper into that argument. I ended up presenting it at an American Political Science Meeting.

The reason this is relevant to my thoughts today is that Heidegger was a Nazi. Not just an anti-Semite, a proclaimed Nazi.

That didn't hinder me from finding a lot of solace, inspiration and thinking (if you know Heidegger you understand the pun) in his work. Equally, one of my constant philosophical interlocutors, who I encountered in a close reading course also in my Masters was Nietzsche, who was neither sympathetic to Jews nor to women.

So, from an early stage I realised that for me engaging texts, or cultural artefacts generally, was a process I underwent distinctly from my moral and political judgement. Something could be fascinating or galvanising and written by someone whose opinions I abhor (or in Heidegger's case, whose work threatened my community directly).

I had been pondering all this while living in the USA in 2016–2017. I saw how the culture wars began, and how moralising became the taste of the day. You had to love only culture that corresponded to your values, and you couldn't consume anything written by someone who might have created something vaguely offensive. Of course, I'm simplifying things and pastiching them, but that was certainly the mood in discussions of culture.

We are all products of complex networks. And where I find my strongest opposition to the interleaving of morality, politics and culture to create a deterministic set of preferences, is that the owl of Minerva flies at dusk. We simply do not know how history will pan out with regards to various things we believe in, and also, no one is right about everything, all of the time. Not even you, reader, who thinks that you are! I certainly have changed my mind, to and fro, over the past two months, and beyond that, not least because the context of our thinking constantly changes. Should we pick one sentence or utterance that didn't cohere with what we wish to see as progressive values and decide that voice is now not worthy of listening?

I don't want to pile on about "cancel culture", which means in essence still participating in said culture wars, and amplifying the right-wing voices that seek to shut down any progress. But, progress and historical shifts occur through dialectics, through opposites, and without knowing what we're up against, what are the things that make us who we were and who we are, we can't aspire towards who we wish to be.

I thought of all this while humming Yoni Rechter, and thinking of my years in the UK and US, in which while declaring I'm a lefty Israeli I was expected by proxy to show I'm a self-hating Jew, or maybe a self-hating Israeli, which has less of a ring to it. To hate all the texts in which I was raised, as they were products of a dark society (so I was told), that everything around me was part of brainwashing, corrupt, and unworthy of respect or even affection. I don't think I ever discussed what I was reading or listening to at home with friends abroad.

I also remember finding on my mother's bookshelf Virginia Woolf's *A Room of One's Own*, and finding that mind-blowing. I remember reading Gideon Levy's weekly column from the age of twelve or thirteen, a column in which he chronicled the horrors of the occupation and apartheid. I had seen it all in Israeli culture, the good, the bad and the ugly, and not least, understood it was part of who I was. Don't get me wrong, there are plenty of things I hate about myself, like everyone else, but somehow the songs, texts and feelings of my hinterlands became safe from self-loathing. I am immensely critical of how culture can be weaponised to exclude and to oppress. But, I assure you, Yoni

Rechter's songs aren't that!

I think this ability to hold on to who I am, and to complexity around me—and we are all products of the cultural texts we are raised upon, all of them—gives me strength and courage to work and speak both with people abroad but also with Israelis. In order to change public opinion you have to, at least, not hate the culture from which you come, and to be able to speak to people around you, even when you disagree. To bring any change and any shift away from the occupation and apartheid no doubt major work is necessary among Israelis. So not hating myself, and not hating all of us, is perhaps also very effective for any campaigning.

Over the past few months I've been listening to Chava Alberstein, another beloved Israeli singer-songwriter, who turned 77 last week. This made me disproportionately happy for her, and for us as her music was all over social media. One song especially has become my anthem since 7th October, to the lyrics of poet Tirza Atar (Nathan Alterman's daughter). It is called "Sometimes the night is songs". It has the beautiful phrase: sometimes the night is a prayer for a different tomorrow. I continue to hold on to that, and to the texts who made me who I am, for better or worse.

12.12.2023

## The uses and abuses of hope

My beloved, late great feminist philosopher mentor at Oxford, Pamela Anderson (yes, she laughed at that coincidence herself, too) used to say proudly "I'm a feminist and a Kantian!". At times

I still return to that statement and ponder it. Like many things that Pam said and wrote it held more complexity that can be apparent at first sight. But I found myself thinking about that statement, and specifically, about Kant's question regarding what we may hope for? I also recall Jonathan Lear's excellent book, *Radical Hope*, which brought me back to that question from a different perspective, that of indigenous people in the USA whose culture and personhood was attacked so violently, that their hopes had to transcend reality as they had known it when Lear was chronicling their stories. It is a wonderful book I was glad to come across, many years ago, when spending a semester at Northwestern University. Even then it resonated with me in surprising ways and I find myself drawn to it in different moments.

As I had written here I am back with reading Walter Benjamin, who unravels an altogether different kind of hope, or perhaps temporality; the messianic force in his understanding of history. I've been reading some Benjamin while lighting my Hanukkah candles. This year, it's clear to me what every home in Israel is praying for when lighting the candles, as do I: for the safe return of all hostages. After some of the hostages were released, and shared their experiences, the urgency of this became apparent; from maltreatment, malnutrition to general unfathomable anxiety, it is clear no human being should be in this situation. The fact that many children and women who had become symbols of the campaign to release hostages have come home had changed the tone of the campaign. So the feeling of the need to bring them all back, and not to leave anyone behind, has become more urgent to me.

Meanwhile, I prayed for Israel's attacks against Gaza to stop, and wondered how much longer we as a collective can witness and bear this violence. The reporting coming out of Gaza is horrific. In addition to Israeli attacks, the fact that there is scarcity of food, and diseases are spreading fast, means that there are multiple causes of fatality on the Strip. The fact that death by starvation is so near to us, an hour outside of Tel Aviv, is unfathomable, which is why we must pause on it and reflect about it.

I was thinking of all this, while reading Benjamin and staring at my candles, not managing to find much joy in them, and ever scrambling for solace. And I was feeling increasingly angry at myself and those around me for abusing hope. Why must I hope that my fellow countrymen are safe at home? Why must I hope that my country stops this cruel attack against a civilian population, in my name? Surely these are matters for action, not prayer, or hope?

There is something that unites staunch lefties and religious people; the reliance on some external force that is meant to bring redemption. At the start of this war there was a huge wave of volunteering. This is still ongoing, in different guises. I think much of it is the need of us here, implicated in every element of this bloody war, to take some kind of action. Sitting at home and hoping for the best feels offensive at this point.

Then again, I am also pondering the limits of hope, and how we may aspire beyond it. We are not the indigenous people who have to defend their right to hope beyond the present, yet the fact that present times are stifling our imaginations is apparent wherever I look. All my life I've believed that we are all affected by oppression, oppressors and oppressed, not equally, but mutually. The political imagination regarding Israel/Palestine feels particularly stunted at the moment. The fact that the international self-declared radical left is rallying around the slogan "ceasefire now" shows how little we are able to hope beyond just simply returning to a bloody status quo. We know full well a seventeen-year-old siege on Gaza cannot be denied when events unfolding over the past two months are discussed. Whereas nothing can justify the heinous acts of Hamas on the 7th October, we can understand them. Hopelessness, decades, nearly centuries of hopelessness, that drives human beings to commit such acts.

Hope does not depend on mental exercises or empathy. We don't have to stretch ourselves to imagine life as another person, something none of us can anyway do; we live our life through our own life story, and inevitably everything else is coloured through our unique narrative. But we can try and push ourselves to hope beyond what is offered to us, both as individuals and collectives. We can push the world, and Israelis and Palestinians, both, not to depend on messianic forces to redeem us, be they the force of world history or god (if she exists, we could use her right now). We can focus our energies on conjuring all we have for generative action, to push leadership for solutions, not only ceases of fire; we have the right to hope for better. All of us. We have the right to hope for peace, for a life not structured by violence, whether enacting it or suffering it. We have a right to hope for a life outside of endless fear of revenge. We have the right to hope for a future we can't even imagine, but we have the right to demand imagining it. We cannot retreat into the self; if there's one thing that being a feminist and Kantian means to me, it's seeing the enmeshing of morality in the circles in which we are embedded. It is easy to feel fatigued and overwhelmed, but equally it is helpful to remember we cannot afford to stop pushing for this different, more far-reaching hope inscribing a different future. Many people in Gaza, an hour away from me, are now hoping to survive another day. Many people have lost that hope. It is our duty, we, who have time and space for contemplating, to hold that demand for a different hope. We cannot let our hope be abused by sitting around when heinous crimes are done around us, or even in our name. We can use our force for action and hope, truly, for something we don't even know, but will be just, and peaceful.

13.12.2023

## Living in absence

Just before the war broke out, and before I had gone abroad, I visited a small yet beautifully curated Giacometti exhibition in Tel Aviv. I had chatted to a friend about how we both make the point to go to see museums when abroad, yet miss so much culture when it is on our doorstep. So, one Saturday I took myself to walk around this exhibition, thinking that had I been in NY or London or Berlin or Paris, I would have made the point to see it.

I love Giacometti's figures, uneven in texture, minute in material and mass, yet so impressive and evocative. The long, twisted torsos and legs invoke movement in me when I watch them. His figurines to me embody one of the most haunting and mesmerising dialectics, that of presence and lack, being and absence. His figurines are both there and not there, present and absent, the space around the fragile, long structures just as important as the material that forms the sculpture.

I thought about that exhibition and Giacometti's work recently. First, as it is one of many markers of a world I longer inhabit; the world before 7th October. Museums are slowly opening here in Israel but many great pieces are stored underground in what is termed "war procedure". Others, such as this entire exhibition, were hastily shipped abroad in order to protect them. But more deeply, I was thinking of myself walking around those half-present absent figures, and how I have been feeling lately that I had become one of them.

During war, death and grief are constant markers of absence. It is hard to count and mark all those who are no longer here. Our psyche can't really process that. We are trapped in limbo between presence and absence. We are here, but many people aren't. We are physically present yet as defined as the space around us, the immense vacancy, all those who are missing, as we are by our embodied presence. When I go to dance classes these days it almost feels offensive to occupy a body when so many around me have been denied that. This is the greatest marker of difference and distinction now; those who are here and those who are not.

Then there are those who are in limbo. The missing. The kidnapped. Those people disappeared into reserve duty. When news of the kidnappings broke out some families said they'd rather know their loved ones were dead. I get that. Not only the fear of torture and harm inflicted upon them, but an unequivocal demarcating line between here and not here. They are dead.

Gone. Cannot return as strange ghosts.

And then there are the intentional absences. The people of Gaza. Israeli media still brings little or no reporting of life of the 2.2 million people living there, nor of the effects of the Israeli attacks on them. I try not to think of the horrors inflicted on my name, and yet I know I must. The constant seeking of that which is made absent for me makes me remember the manifold violence of making people absent from me, of not letting us all know what the world is watching with horror. It is as if the Gaza Strip is one of those spaces carved around Giacometti's sculptures, evacuated from its physical presence, yet the most important thing. And yet, the Gaza Strip is a real place where women and men and children are desperately trying to survive, against attacks invoked in my name. They are physical beings, not metaphors, not symbols, not pawns.

Yesterday it rained very hard at night. Rain in Israel/Palestine has become fairly unusual, thus an event to mark. I lit the sixth candle of Hanukkah as blazing thunder rang around me. I had pondered the fact that the noise felt uncannily similar to the bombing planes that constantly fly around. We had become so fatigued we got accustomed to living with these heavy bangs structuring our lives.

I had thought of Gaza in the rain. I thought about all those photos I had seen online, of families escaping into makeshift refuges. Those refuges have probably collapsed. How the already precarious structures in which those feeling their homes are hiding must be collapsing under nature's assault. About the fact that whereas this region is so thirsty for rain, now it is not a blessing but a curse. The rain joins Israeli assaults. How does it feel when you sense everything, even nature, is stacked against you? What odds do you have to survive?

Today the rain has ceased but the wind is vicious. The sky is grey. We had heard of eight Israeli soldiers killed in attacks. I saw a touching photo of an orphaned Israeli child, about four, looking at her dead father's photo in the newspaper. People in Gaza don't get to mourn their dead, they don't even get to survive. All our lives have become absent, we are marked by constant puncturing of the space around us, of living beings who become air. It will take us a long time to feel present again, in any substantial way, and to give embodiment and material to make all that has been made absent a new life. I cannot even imagine this process starting to unfold yet I eagerly await that moment.

14.12.2023

## A tale of two bulldozers

Yesterday I heard that the son of a flamenco teacher I once studied with, was killed in Gaza while he was on reserve duty. I remember growing up, when Israel was entrenched in Lebanon, and every few days some soldiers were killed. It is such a horrific routine, and it is returning to us. Meanwhile I'm reading more and more about starvation and diseases in Gaza. In addition to the indiscriminate bombardment, people living in inhumane conditions are suffering unimaginable consequences of this lengthy assault, enacted by my government, in my name. I know it sounds naive, but I just want everything to stop.

A few weeks ago, I had a chat with a dear friend and a brilliant international lawyer I have long admired. We discussed the events of the 7th October, and she said, her eyes shining: when I saw the bulldozer coming through the wall, I was so overjoyed. This is something I had heard from a variety of people, before we learnt the consequences of Hamas's horrific attacks and the extent of the war crimes committed then. The image of a bulldozer coming through the fence was heroic. Hearing this from her gave me permission to ponder it myself; I had felt so many conflicting emotions about this day. By the time I had seen this image, I knew more about its consequences, yet its force is undeniable. Those living in a large open-air prison breaking free, defying their oppressors.

Personally, that image evoked different memories and emotions for me. In May 2022, as Director of Peace Now, we (Peace Now) hired a bulldozer and went to demolish the illegal outpost of Homesh. Homesh is one of the most violent outposts, sitting on private Palestinian land, especially of the village of Burqa. Very often when the army witnesses attacks by violent settlers, a method to acquire land and intimidate people off their property, it does nothing or even joins in the attacks. Palestinians living in Burqa are under constant terror. The Supreme Court hardly offers respite, as it consistently rules in favour of the settlers as in cases in East Jerusalem I had written about previously.

Around April, I got a phone call from friends in the NGO Yesh Din, which represents the people of Burqa in their long legal battle to hold on to their lands. The Palestinians in Burqa are keen to do something with Israeli activists, they said. This is unusual as many refuse to engage Israelis at all, let alone Peace Now, which has "Zionist" in its title. I took this opportunity with both hands.

One of my staff members came up with this idea: as the Supreme Court and the army do nothing, we'll hire a bulldozer and say we will demolish the outpost of Homesh. I chatted to people I trust. Everyone said it was brilliant. We had a plan.

Of course, it was illegal, from start to finish. Citizens can't hire a bulldozer and take action against constructions, even if those are illegal in themselves. Ordinary citizens can't take action instead of the indecisive and criminal state. But, knowing the army's conduct in the West Bank, we knew we wouldn't be let anywhere close to the outpost, and this was a performative action anyway.

My biggest fear, perhaps surprising to you, was of conservative forces around me. Peace Now's board is very old and conservative. They had been anyway driving me crazy, with demands and ideas hurled at me from 7am till 11pm. I knew they'd hate the idea. So, I decided not to tell them. I told them we're planning an action, but just didn't share what it was. Meanwhile, we were also careful not to leak the plan to the police. We never discussed it around mobile phones and verified all activists who wished to be in the loop.

The thing that gave me confidence more than anything was a solidarity visit to Burqa in which we shared our idea with Palestinians in danger of losing their land. We sat around the table, a couple of activists and me, with a variety of people: community leaders, released prisoners, farmers who lost their land to violent settler attacks. They had all said: this is great. For years Israelis were just talking about peace and coexistence. At last you're doing something.

We found a bulldozer driver who was willing to go along with the plan and released a massive campaign around it. It resonated strongly. The Israeli right was alarmed; I went on various news interviews and talk shows to explain and defend the action. The board, predictably, was furious, though at this point we were getting so much interest and traction they were pleased about that and honestly: I didn't care. The point of the action was achieved already: the illegality of Homesh and the violent attacks suffered by Palestinians there were all over the news.

On the day of the action, we set out, bulldozer in tow. We had arranged to meet up before crossing the border into the West Bank. A few activists were arrested en route, so we knew we were bugged and followed by Israeli police. In the parking lot in which we had arranged to meet, suddenly undercover cops arrived and arrested the bulldozer driver, a Palestinian citizen of Israel. I told them as I was the one who paid the driver, hence instigating the supposed crime, they should arrest me. Then all hell broke loose. We managed to get quite a few activists, and we all just sat and stopped the police from proceeding with the bulldozer. For more than an hour, we blocked all entrances to the parking lot, and the police were stuck with us. After an hour they called for backup and we were removed, the driver taken into custody. We sent lawyers and he was released swiftly and without any charges. Meanwhile, we went on our buses and drove to the Burqa area. Our contacts there had offered us all sorts of secret roundabout ways to reach them without police noticing us, but we chose to use the main roads. We were there to defy the state, not escape it. We got not far from Burqa and were stopped once more, this time by the Israeli army. We protested for a bit and then went home.

This was on all news editions: when I got home my mother

texted me and said "I saw you on the 5 o'clock news fighting with the police". We knew we wouldn't be able to demolish Homesh, but we wanted to raise awareness to the injustice there, and that we achieved.

I had recounted all this to my friend, and in my mind, as the bulldozer coming through Gaza's wall started circulating in my feeds. I can now, with distance, and without thinking about the horrific acts committed after the bulldozer came through the wall, understand why it had brought so much joy around the world. We now have a rich hindsight and those who still do not connect this image to what we know about the 7th October and its consequences are suspect to me. I understand how and why those people suffering so much structural violence under apartheid, for so long, would want to break through walls imprisoning them. In a way, that is what I tried to do in solidarity, a year ago. And so, our goal, as societies, is to ensure that bulldozers aren't necessary, that people care enough about injustice and settler violence and denial of freedom of movement so that these dramatic acts are unnecessary. Until then, we hold on to those two images, and keep kindling hope for the people of Burqa and Gaza, both.

16.12.2023

## The endless swirl of heartache: calling to prioritise life over death

I find myself looking forward to my Fridays. Yesterday I woke up with a strange burst of inexplicable anxiety. Things are terrible, all the time, so these bursts send me into endless questioning of their source. I took my ballet class, which was a respite, at least, for my brain, then I went to meet a dear friend and join a chat with dancers reflecting on their art since 7th October. I had mainly wanted to see my friend, so tagged along; though it was interesting listening to the very young dancers talk sensitively and gently about confusion and loss. There was much gentleness in the air, something appreciated in its own right. Then I went, like every Friday since the war started, to Sipur Pashut; my favourite for its denizens: wonderful women who never cease to supply me with thought-provoking conversations, book recommendations, probing questions, hugs, intense existential debates and baked goods, not necessarily in that order. I find these afternoons a mainstay of my week, and I always return with books I hadn't planned to read, which in turn I discover I love. Find people who give you books you don't know you'll love, you'll see how rich your life will become.

The day progressed, and I threw myself into reading, though the ball of anxiety had refused to disappear from my stomach. It all felt heavy and impossible to escape. How many weeks have we been enduring this? and how many more are yet to come? The uncertainty was overbearing. I read and read. Among other reasons, I'm investing in books as I find pushing myself to read and having a good pile of books I want to start on, sends me away from doom scrolling and/or becoming too immersed in internet arguments.

I had planned to go to sleep early, and then the news broke; three hostages were accidentally killed by the Israeli army. It felt so hopeless; without any clear intentions of this military operation. "Destroying Hamas" is so vague, and now becoming more and more apparent: impossible, the hefty civilian death toll is becoming impossible to stomach and contain.

Of course, the death toll on the Palestinian side has been horrendous, and unfathomably high. The Israeli army is strong, too strong, and its attacks are now genocidal in consequence even if not in intent. However, I am Israeli, and the news of more civilian casualties from my community sent my heart spiralling down in heaviness.

Many of us say that if we choose violence and death, we will end up paying the price ourselves. This is a classic campaigning formulation. If you tolerate cruelty it will return to you. Now, many of us who use this slogan in different iterations know full well it's not always true. There are people who lead a life of cruelty and yet their own private being is protected and safe from harm. Collectives can get away with murder, literally, and their lives can be made distinct from their violent actions. One can argue that morally, investing many resources in sustaining a regime of structural violence will inevitably affect distributions of resources internally and corrupt the society from within. We, on the Israeli left, have been arguing this for decades. Yet, it's impossible to deny that in many respects, Israel has enjoyed impunity for its actions, and the price of oppression does not always crystallise itself in the everyday life of liberal middle-class Israelis such as myself.

But, the event of yesterday has shifted that conversation. In the conscious choice of continuing this murderous and indiscriminate attacks on Gaza we are killing our own people. My thoughts after hearing the news went to the soldiers who fought there, in Shuja'iyya, and will have carried out this attack. How can you live with yourself after this? How can you hold the pain, and guilt, of executing so much violence, including against your own people?

There are videos circulating of Israeli soldiers committing various heinous attacks and crimes, sabotaging and vandalising Palestinian private property.. When discussing war crimes, ultimately the responsibility of those rests with those who give orders. My friends, colleagues, friends' partners and family members are entrenched in the fighting in Gaza execute policy, rather than form it. Some of them are lefty activists. So, all these dissonances circled through my mind, as well as the families of these hostages who had got this awful news.

The Israeli leadership is constantly choosing death over life. Many of us feel deeply the pain of watching Palestinian casualties' numbers escalate in such numbers. Many of us also spend our days worrying about friends and relatives fighting in Gaza. To be an Israeli Jew or Druze means that you always hold more than one narrative, that you can both condemn the actions of the army and worry desperately for people you know who are there. And now I find myself also worrying for the day after the war: for the return of those soldiers, traumatised and broken, into our society. How can we look into a different future? How can we hope that this horror doesn't continue or even repeat itself?

For that, we must call for prioritising life over death. For the sake of all of us. I do not want to see any more Palestinian dead, killed "to make me safe". I know full well my safety won't be achieved through mass murder and destruction. But also, I want to protect my community. Living in the UK taught me, on a very profound and visceral level, that I will not have any other home apart from this complex piece of land. This is where I belong, for better or worse. When the heartache is overwhelming, I remind myself that it is my duty to alleviate it for those around me, and put every effort I can to make this place a better homeland for all of us, Palestinians and Israelis, through deliberation and care rather than endless war.

Since yesterday I've been feeling that my heart is in an endless swirling freefall. It feels as if there is a void under my feet that had broken down, and there is endless space opening around me holding this ever-expanding hurt. But today I'll go and protest to raise my voice for a ceasefire, a hostage exchange deal, and equal rights for all between the river and the sea. This is my home and it is my duty to do what I can to care for it, so that it becomes a place of justice and peace, and calling it home won't feel so heavy as it does now.

18.12.2023

## Hunger, hate

There are many bits of news that are circling in my mind, and I am trying to repress, or discuss with people I appreciate, or place in context, yet they refuse to be obedient; they come up at unexpected moments and haunt my thoughts. One such fact is the crisis of nourishment and food in Gaza. The denial of aid into Gaza means that people are now starving en masse, some of them to death.

The Israeli argument states that Hamas is the one which is

denying the access to aid, harming its own citizens. At this point, I do not care if this is true or not. There are people living an hour's drive from me who are starving to death. Of all the horrors of this war, that's one I find impossible to fathom, deeply.

The thing about living through this hell—it's been ten weeks—is that it both changes who we are and feeds into who we are. When people ask me gently how I'm doing, and how I'm able to get through this period, the simple answer is that none of us have any choice and we can only choose the resources with which we are provided.

Yesterday morning I chatted with my new colleagues whom I adore, and have known before I started this job, all of whom are good feminist comrades. I can't remember in which context, but I shared my experiences of working in dance when I was in my mid-20's. I was mainly teaching but also performing, and dance was my entire orbit for a couple of years. It was a complicated time for me. I weighed fifteen kilos less than I do today. I was deeply unhealthy. My periods had stopped and I found myself in the emergency room more than once. This wasn't intentional; it was a result of working too hard and my body being completely unprepared for what I had been doing.

I really love dance, yet I always joke that it is a one-sided relationship. I am not very good at it, yet have learnt, with age, to let go and just enjoy dance class for the sake of movement itself.

Yesterday I had shared some of the stories of my time in dance with my colleagues, who were shocked and appalled. The attitude towards the body and hunger and food is extremely unhealthy in the world of dance. Yet, with time I looked around me and saw it was only the extreme of what I was seeing in so many women.

There are few women, I think, who haven't experienced eating disorders of some form or another. Be it a short and extreme diet or addiction to sport to maintain a specific body type or bingeing and then feeling guilty. At some point you learn to let go, or realise life is more than your body, but for none of us is this a simple relationship.

Yesterday I had told my colleagues one story that stayed with me: when I worked as a dance teacher, a woman I worked with made me stand in front of the younger dancers in leotard and tights and said: look, this is how a dancer looks. I was very underweight and unhealthy and had been made an example for others for that.

We've all felt heartbroken since the weekend. I went on a series of demonstrations: first there was one against the government, then one calling for a ceasefire, then one calling for the hostages to return. The political complexities here mean that they are separate demonstrations despite, for me, completely overlapping in their call.

I met a colleague from the human rights world, who's been in this line of work for decades. I really look up to her. I have never seen her as distraught as when she was talking about the Israeli army shooting the hostages. And I've seen her speak harshly about the Israeli army so many times. We discussed this, and other things, and it remained with me throughout Sunday.

In the evening I went to my ballet class. I started taking it in pointe shoes, as a challenge for myself. I'm not doing very well and I'm not very good at it, and yesterday my teacher, Gabrielle who is absolutely lovely, asked me to try something more difficult.

I said I couldn't and just gave up, swirling into a dramatic hyperbolic whirlwind of anxiety and sadness.

Before the class I had seen my former studio choreographer in the waiting room, the one who had made me stand in front of the class and waxed lyrical about my extremely unhealthy body. Israel is a tiny country, and the dance community is even smaller, so this is not such a strange coincidence, yet it felt odd I had spoken about her, and that time in my life, just that morning.

And so, I felt frustrated, sad, and extremely privileged and stupid for engaging these thoughts: my ballet class, my body, when people are starving an hour away from me.

When I was in the UK I worked for a while with a feminist body image campaigning group. I broke off with it finally because of its lack of ability to deal with social-economic issues. Attitude to food in the UK, and all around the world, really, is organised around social class and generally, your relationship with your body depends not only on learnt habits but on what you can afford. In my years in the UK I was always horrified by the price and low quality of vegetables, and the fact that eating a healthy, well-balanced diet, truly was a privilege.

It's also fairly obvious that if you have time to obsess about your body, to engage in physical activity to shape it, to reflect on your relationship to it you are privileged. You have time, and resources, to invest in all those activities. If you're trying to survive, these are thoughts that don't occupy your mind.

I was thinking of all this, walking home after a really bad ballet class, contemplating how women's relationship to food and how we're taught to internalise this self-hate, denial of indulgence, and generally frugality and abstention from desire, is part of the same axis through which we turn a blind eye to hunger, other-inflicted hunger, when it occurs in our midst.

Poverty and hunger are clearly not only happening in Gaza. The economic situation in Israel itself is in dire straits since the war; the poor are getting poorer, the hungry are getting hungrier. We are taught to focus on ourselves as some kind of project to develop, our bodies being part of that. We learn through western white socialisation to understand ourselves as separate, not implicated in each other. The fact that I will eat more, we learn, will not cost anyone to eat less. And we learn to form a relationship between hatred and hunger, internalise what the world thinks of us in denying food from ourselves, when people are actually begging to survive would pray for any of the foods we deny ourselves.

Of all the things that scare me about this war, I am worried about how we are going to get through the hatred. I'm not talking about the hatred turned to us, but the hatred we, Israelis, are holding within us. The fact that we can go through life with people starving an hour from us, and yet do our shopping, live, eat, feel different things about our bodies. There is a deep internalised hatred here, a feeling of unworthiness, lack of humanity of other people, which we are able to endure, that scares me. The question of hunger and Gaza returns to me every day. I've escaped one world in which I was taught how to hate myself and be hungry in order to be beautiful. Now I want to escape this world I'm currently living in and live in a world in which we are all moved by wanting safe and fair access to food instead of hatred, so deep that it harms others' bodies while we go on about our lives.

Apparently Netanyahu wants to change the name of this war, signalling it will go on for a while. The name he's interested in is Genesis. And I could only think of this quote, which summarises how I feel: "the earth was formless and empty, darkness over the surface of the deep."

21.12.2023

## Reading/reaching beyond the horizon

The number of dead in Gaza is nearing 20,000 people. Another Israeli soldier in my orbit was killed; the brother-in-law of a friend from dance. Every day we hear of several other military casualties, while hearing that the north of the Strip has been put under the Israeli army's control. There are rumours of another humanitarian pause and hostage exchange deal. Nothing has been confirmed.

Yesterday I went to see dance with a dear friend. It was a beautiful performance that took me in an endless, breathless swirl along with the dancers. It was intense and just what I needed at this moment exactly. I took a taxi home, and the Palestinian taxi driver said to me: those who died go to a better place, right? they have to be somewhere better. I couldn't argue with him.

Since the start of the war I've been reading incessantly. Luckily, I'm good with reading when anxious; in fact, I read best in the worst of times. And so, I've been devouring anything I can: fiction, non-fiction, philosophy, politics, poetry.

Right now I'm reading, in addition to a novel by the inimitable Jacqueline Kahanoff, two books that send me away from the grim here and now, though not necessarily to escape to better places.

When I was in the UK in October I picked up in Piccadilly Waterstones Olivia Laing's *The Lonely City*. I had read some of her non-fiction and loved it; *Funny Weather* was a chance buy at Shakespeare & Company, the only store on par with Sipur Pashut for me in terms of emotional connection for it. Laing's work on loneliness, and especially the avant garde artists of NYC's experience seeping into their work, has proven a very good companion for this moment for me. First, Laing (who herself is non-binary) focuses on queer art and artists, something I feel really necessary for me at this moment. The war is an assault on women in many ways, but the war is also an assault on anything that is not heteronormative. We are all reduced to being wives, sisters, mothers and partners of men in combat, and those of us who are not wives or mothers of men, and have not aspired to this lifestyle, or do not wish to see men in combat, feel very much outside of discourse at the moment—a different form of loneliness. I have gravitated intentionally towards queer writing, not least, as it provides a challenge to this uniform and unchallenged perception of womanhood and women's place in society. Laing's writing on Andy Warhol, David Wojjnarowictz, Valerie Solanas, Henry Darger and others has been a lifeline away from my feeling of descent; not only have we all descended into a dark timeline in which hope for any action that is not military is scarce; we are now, all, recruited and drafted for this bloody war (pun intended) and for that there is only one form of womanhood accepted.

At the same time, I am reading poetry translated from Persian from modern Iran by Orly Noy. Orly is one of those women whom I both adore and admire in equal measure. We first met in a demonstration in Sheikh Jarrah and continued the conversation over multiple chats. I have always felt we could talk forever and on the other hand that she has endless insight and wisdom I can feed off. One of the nice perks of my current job is that Orly is a longstanding editor and writer for *Local Call* and so I get to hang out with her. Orly is the chair of the board for B'tselem, by far Israel's biggest and most influential human rights organisation. She is also an active member of Balad, a Palestinian party calling for equal rights for all citizens. Her activism makes her a target for much vitriol and hatred, yet she carries her politics and ideology with unparalleled grace and gravity. She's also very amusing and good fun to be around. Orly was born in Iran, thus is one of the only voices here bringing reporting and commentary from that corner of the world, including much-needed comparisons between events unfolding there and here. Among other things, she notes that the dissent in Iran has been far larger and overarching than here in Israel, despite much more at stake.

I've been thinking of languages lately. I wrote this book in English thinking of an international readership, but working now also in Hebrew has been very comforting and good for my soul, and I'm reading more and more books in Hebrew. Both my mother and aunt are translators by vocation. Their first language was German, not Hebrew; they picked up Hebrew in primary school. They both studied in Geneva and spoke French between them so that I wouldn't understand as a child, and German to my grandmother for the same reason (which means I pushed myself and tried and now can pretty much follow German and French so that I could understand all those things hidden from me). I learnt Arabic in school and picked up a lot of extra layers of it just from living here, between the river and the sea. My father never managed to learn Hebrew, and much of my childhood I translated for him when he needed it. My mother and aunt looked down on him for speaking only one language, and equally looked down on me for speaking only two. They still do, rightly so.

One of the things I missed while living in the UK is having access to more translations. So much of the literary universe in the anglophone world is, well, anglophone, I really waited for my breaks at home to read anything that is not British or American. And so, having access, including an introduction and annotation, to poetry from Iran feels like an unusually generous boon. The poems are beautiful, and many dark—something that resonates with this moment, but just rich in language and metaphor and imagery that is so different yet so profound for me to access.

And so, I find myself intentionally reading, or reaching, beyond my horizons beyond this moment, which feels constantly assaulting me in these boundaries of what is possible, to what we might hope, what we need to think about and to whom we can compare ourselves. There are constant limitations on our imaginations: on what we might strive towards, what are the possibilities, from different places, in different spaces and in different languages to escape this very dark moment. I would not survive this time without books and bookish people. So if you've been my reader and we discussed books, or writing, over the past three months; this is a warm thank you to you. And now, back to work, as having good books await me makes me focused on my never-ending to do list.

## Stopping/presence

First, a technical disclaimer; I know most of the world is breaking off for Christmas today, but I'll keep writing here; for one, we don't have any time off, and a lot of things are happening at the same time.

Today I went to a ballet class (as ever), which was lovely; the teacher brought us all chocolates in honour of Christmas, and I even enjoyed the adagio. Then, as every Friday, I went to Sipur Pashut; we read some poetry by the inimitable and recently departed poet Amira Hess by opening a book randomly. Yet all the poems we found felt very poignant for this moment. I was thinking of Merce Cunningham's chance operations; maybe there is more intention in chance than we know... Then I went to a protest action for the hostages. The hostages have kind of lost the front headlines here. The immense death toll in Gaza, as well as the fact that some have returned, have made the situation more complex. Also, the gender element has become complicated; many women and children had returned, now there are young and old men, mostly, who comprise the majority of the hostages. Somehow the call to bring back "women and children" was easier for some to stomach, yet again showing the gendered element of this war, and every war. The action today was organised by Merav Svirsyi, an artist whose parents were both killed on the 7th October and whose brother is still held as a hostage in Gaza. I stood right behind her the whole time and thought of the sheer wretchedness of this situation. Can you imagine your family member being held captive and you, a citizen, have to mobilise and remind your government of its obligations towards you and your family? It's just so awful. The action was organised in solidarity with some prominent dance people, and there was a good turnout (pun intended) of the dance community, which was nice. The idea of the action was to walk very, very slowly up a central boulevard in Tel Aviv. No phones, no speaking, just slow walking.

The action felt weirdly meditative. At the beginning the organiser said that if at any point anyone wants to leave they can just depart, yet I noticed no one did. For two hours, we just walked slowly holding photos of the hostages and a banner that said: "Stopping everything! Bringing them back". We were briefed not to answer back if there is an opposition, yet I was surprised and delighted that not much of that arose. One American shouted at us loudly that "We are the reason they're there", with increasing tones and volume, but he was quickly pushed aside by passers-by. One taxi driver shouted something about "not protesting while soldiers are dying" but he was fairly calm (far more than the American dude). And, despite the action being intentionally disruptive; we had blocked the boulevard for a length of time, people around us found ways to walk by us and many said encouraging things when they were doing so. I have to confess I'm not used to such positive and generous reception of protest; this made me think that the hostages are probably more consensual than most issues in Israeli society right now, and that if a public opinion poll would have suggested to stop the war and bring hostages back this would have won a large majority. I guess that's why this question isn't asked.

During the march I walked by my ballet teacher Gabrielle and another local choreographer I know, but no one spoke. I had pondered the question of presence. First, a working assumption; in our digital world presence is never just physical presence. Half of this war is taking place on social media and on the internet and engaging it in real life is accompanied by engaging it online. Checking out: either from real life, or from the internet, means you'll always have half of the image. The discourse around the war, and actions such as I participated in today, arise by and large on social networks. My own engagement with social media is very much inspired by Eleanor Marx and Rosa Luxemburg, both of whom adopted early on new technologies and understood that political life will refer to them, whether we like it or not.

I've been looking at posts that make me feel uncomfortable, intentionally; not of American influencers who tell me what to think, but of Palestinians and Israelis who are mobilising and thinking and taking different paths to mine. I can never guess what they're thinking, and I don't have to; now it's all online. In a similar way that overhearing an uncomfortable argument will still draw us in, I'm following to the best of my ability what is happening around me, whether I agree with it or not. Moreover, in this war, so much has unravelled on social media; be it the Instagrammers from Gaza or Leila Moran, the British Palestinian MP who live tweeted from a church in Gaza that was under Israeli attack. So being present on social media has been key. Also, and on a personal note, so many of you are writing and supporting via those networks, and it makes life so much nicer and easier. One can't always write lengthy emails to everyone; these essays started out of that assumption, but also, social media is an effective in-between method of communication.

And then there is real life presence. I've been feeling lately people are really hungry to be together at this moment, no matter the missile alarms and other challenges. Tel Aviv feels strangely full. People go to all sorts of events. There is something about togetherness in person which is just so invaluable. So whereas certainly social media is essential to both understand and organise within the war, for comfort and solidarity in-person events are truly singular. I feel really bad for Israeli friends who are missing all that from abroad; and often feel I am attending with them in mind and heart.

At the beginning of this war I got many generous offers (if you, reader, were one of those who made them, thank you again) of a place to stay and hide during the war. I was touched by the extent of them (I could have done an around-the-world tour had I accepted all!) yet I felt very firmly I need to be here. I understand why some people left, yet as one friend with dual nationality said to me, not everyone has the privilege to go, and if they can't, why should I? and so, I feel really rooted, really present where I am right now. I know full well the space around me is unjust and for any viable political solution that would enable not only the end of this war but stopping the future ones, it will have to change dramatically and include people who've been displaced and chased away from the land while excluded from our shared spaces. But this is where I was brought up and this is my home, whether in good times or in very bad ones. In a strange way, I feel those of us who have been running to the shelters together, going on marches together, holding bring the hostages back signs together, crying when soldiers' names are announced together, have created another network of rootedness. I believe that if and when we, Jewish Israelis, are able to understand the wrongs in which our solidarity is rooted, and expand it to others, this place can be truly singular in its goodness. This place can be so beautiful when it is just. Till then we keep fighting. Shabbat shalom; a Shabbat of peace.


23.12.2023


## A Christmas wish from around the corner of a little town of Bethlehem

I have a complicated relationship to Christmas. My father was Christian, and so my entire childhood we celebrated Christmas as well as Hanukkah. I was thinking lately that perhaps the reason I never concede to just one narrative around me is because I was raised with two at least, which never cohered and just were part and parcel of my upbringing and my life. Every year we lit candles and my father played the Hanukkah song Ma'oz Tzur on the piano, and then I would wake up on the 25th December and look at what Father Christmas brought for me. Considering my birthday is also in December, I was just happy for all the festivities and joys.

My father died nearly four years ago. In the first year after his death, it felt offensive to celebrate Christmas. I felt like that part of my calendar was abruptly taken from me, that it was no longer mine. I was angry at those who insisted on wishing me "Happy Christmas". If you have ever grieved for anyone close, you know well the holidays are always hard, regardless of any extra cultural complexity. With time, I let go of the anger, and accepted Christmas back into my life, in a different way. Mainly, I let myself be awash with happy memories of spending time with my family as a child; my father listening to Handel's Messiah, me and my father watching the Nutcracker together. He was a balletomane and was the person who got me hooked on dance. In addition, my years living in a Christian country lent me some new memories: Christmas dinners in my Oxford college, going to carol concerts, drinking mulled wine in Oxford's Christmas market after conducting intense admissions interviews; these were probably my favourite "new" memories. With time I also noticed that many Israelis around me who had lived abroad marked Christmas in one way or another, supermarkets aimed at the Russian immigrant communities were full of decorations and chocolate as the Russian Jews marked "Novi God", a holiday using Christmas themes. So, I let myself take some joy and pleasure in those.

This year, I've heard from different Palestinian Christian friends that their communities are treating Christmas differently. The grief for the death toll in Gaza is tremendous, and the feeling of heaviness is everywhere in Palestinian communities. I told someone I know, a practicing Christian, and he said, "I can understand why you wouldn't feel like celebrating Christmas". I don't think this captures the extent of the decision to not mark Christmas here, and the reason for that.

As part of my disjuncture of an Israeli Jew abroad over Christmas I was always somewhere between amused and confused hearing about sites that I knew from home (yet were not mine) referred to in hymns and readings. I was an excellent caroller at university, and especially loved "O little town of Bethlehem" and chuckled to myself that it's not a little town, it's Palestinian, and nothing like the hymn alluded to. The Christian Palestinian community is smaller than the Muslim one, yet the connection between this land to the sites to which Christians all around the world pray and long has sustained. Flying to Tel Aviv around this time always brought pilgrims and priests of various kinds on my flights. I recall one flight in which around fifty nuns were sitting on the plane, and I felt like an extra in The Sound of Music. I always knew that for various people my homeland was "the Holy Land". I used to sign my emails "regards from the not-very-holy-land" when visiting home.

Yet, the decision to not have grand and open celebrations for Christmas here is a big one. It's not a matter of "not feeling like it". It's protesting on a symbolic plain that constitutes the ontological place in which the narrative of Christmas took place. It's removing the ground, quite literally, from the story of Christmas.

Living abroad added to the complexity of my feelings towards Christmas. I was appalled by the commercial nature of Christmas; most people around me mainly saw it as a time for shopping and a break from work. Very few people took interest in the holiday's meaning and symbols, and even the music and other cultural artifice around it. So, I'm both sad and also not surprised that the little town of Bethlehem is not on many people's minds this year, as they rush for Christmas shopping and take joy in putting their auto-reply on email. And thus even this act of protest, which is really what the Palestinian community has by way of power internationally, is perceived as "not feeling like celebration"; a personal, individualistic act rather than collective dissent. Christmas in Anglo-America resides on a very different sphere than its origins story and development here, in the place that bears the names from which it started. "O little town of Bethlehem" does not feel like a real place and its people not real people, including to those who actually engage with the carol and sing and pray about those places.

Since October 7th we've all been living in disjointed ontologies, referring to different realities, different symbolic orders, defining different facts as crucial and different moments as the beginning of our origin stories. Even before that, Christians internationally no longer referred to Christians here as guardians of the most crucial ontology for them; those places reside in Westernised ontologies, gaining meaning as places outside of their actual geographical locations. It feels like there's multiple "Little towns of Bethlehem". It is sad but not surprising that Christians who don't live here don't really engage the meaning and extent of making this move, or disengaging the symbolic order from where it seems to be at its origins. This order has been severed and even those who practice and sing about the origin story don't think about its real existence.

I wrote yesterday about realising that I need to engage with social media in order to understand this war, how to campaign against it and how to engage with those who disagree with me around it. I've found recently that the people who upset me the most on social media are those who write hollow statements on everything I post, such as "praying for peace" or something of this kind.

Many of whom are also practising Christians. The reality here is so horrendous that I find it offensive to see people cling onto slogans and words that bring them comfort while looking away from the world in all its gore. Of course, peace is what I and many people around me strive towards, but in order to get even close to that, so much healing, restorative justice, and just a deep space of grief have to be held. It feels to me selfish to impose on us this wish coming from a symbolic order held metaphysically, so far from the world in which unborn babies die because they have no access to medical care and children look for their relatives under the rubble in Gaza. Once again, I feel a distanced Christian symbolic order that has little connection to the land and people here is imposed upon it. I found the need to disengage from these people first. Don't talk to me about peace on earth before you're willing to look at the pain and grief people are living through here, in your Holy Land. If I can force myself to look at Gaza Instagrammers' photos of ash-clad children running to look for their families, so should a Christian who wants to see peace in any possible way come to this earth.

I felt heavy hearing of the decision not to have big public events for Christmas yet understood it and felt the need to be in solidarity with it, from my bad-atheist-Jewess-half-Christian point of view. This is a sad Christmas, whether you are interested in what had happened in the "Holy Land" a million years ago, or not; take a stern look at what is happening here now, around the corner from the little town of Bethlehem. My Christmas wish is for a ceasefire to finally be installed and last, for Israel to tend to its injured, dead and grieving, and focus on life not revenge; and Palestinian communities to receive solidarity not only as victims of atrocities but as a people who deserve, like all of us, the right to self-determination and cultural and political sovereignty. My Christmas wish is for us to make the small, important step towards a just peace—recognising and acknowledging power disparities as well as the pain held by all communities on this land. My Christmas wish is that we are able to look at the worlds inhabited around us, and that the world outside of these borders between the river and the sea looks at us and understands we are real people who wish to live, not die, and need solidarity in order to cease this senseless violence. Before more young people die in the Israeli military, before other civilian casualties occur in Gaza, that we live here: Christians, Muslims, Jews, understanding each other's ontologies and symbolic orders, or at least leaving space for not-understanding, and that we can start dreaming of peace while looking straight at our pain, around the corner from the little town of Bethlehem.

24.12.2023

Discussed: "Loving Arabs": on the internal reckoning of the Israeli Jewish left

My favourite dance work on the relationship of Israelis to Palestinians is, by far, Hillel Kogan's "Loving Arabs". It is a pastiche of an Israeli dancer who wants to make a work on co-existence, all cliches in tow, but struggles to find a Palestinian partner with whom to enact his performance. The work is powerful as it's very funny. Kogan uses a lot of text in his work, and he is sophisticated and witty, but it is also sad. It shows the reality of so many people living under apartheid. And the work is profound as it does what art does best: take a stereotype and play with it until it is stretched to its extremes. Kogan tours a lot, and I can recommend watching this work if it gets to you; I won't spoil too much of the work but will say the work ends by Kogan and his Palestinian counterpart sharing hummus with the audience to embody coexistence. The pastiche is also effective as it plays on the classic "my Palestinian friend" which is just another iteration of "my Black friend", or "my Jewish friend" the way people will engage with a singular person to make themselves feel better about themselves.

I saw this work multiple times, and saw it received in multiple ways: from anger (of a mostly Israeli dance teacher audience), to laughter (I took a friend who's the parliamentary assistant to one of the prominent Palestinian members of Knesset to the tenth anniversary of this work, and she laughed so much she wept), and confusion (I saw Kogan once perform the work in the US, where some of the audience didn't realise it was a pastiche, and said it was "amazing" to see Israelis try so hard for coexistence. Sigh.)

Anyway, this work plays on one of the most widespread stereotypes of Israeli lefties, that of us as "Arab lovers", those who prefer other people, in opposition to us as an enemy, more than our own. I had known that stereotype since the beginning of my organising life around 1995; and often contemplated it within myself in conversations around me. One central and unmovable truth I know is that in order to campaign effectively, in order to create change in your community, you must, at the very least, not hate your community. You cannot influence people to change their mind if you feel antagonistic to them, if you feel you're an outsider wishing to "educate" them, if you feel better than your community. They will see you as an outsider and not trust you. This increases threefold in times of crises, in which everyone anyway feels exhausted and vulnerable. No one likes the person who preaches to them, the holier-than-thou, know-it-all, who has cracked how to explain the occupation and apartheid and show you all why they are right, and you are wrong. Rebecca Solnit's excellent *Men Explain Things To Me* comes to mind when reflecting on these approaches.

But, in the most horrid ways, the 7th October was a game changer in the relationship of the Israeli left to the world, to Palestinian comrades, and especially to itself. I don't want to add to the pages written about the international left and us, but rather want to focus on us, the Israeli Jewish leftists, and where we are right now.

The 7th October was an awful game changer because it was an attack on us. Not metaphorically, not virtually, not as a figure of speech. Many pillars of our community were targeted. The cousin of B'tselem's former chair of the board was kidnapped (she returned in the first hostage deal, and now is bravely campaigning to release all hostages and speaks of her time in Gaza). The director of Yesh Din, the most important NGO focusing on settler violence, was in Kfar Aza spending days in the bomb shelter; she lost her sister-in-law in the attack. My friend Yotam Kipnis, an activist in Peace Now who also worked for the mixed community action group Zazim and campaigned in many lefty organisations, as did his parents, lost them both in the attack. And of course,

Vivian Silver z"l. Many of us have family in the south (as do I). This wasn't just an amorphous attack on "us" as a metaphor, it was an attack on our community.

Moreover, in the fighting since then, all of us without exclusion know people fighting in Gaza. Every day I discover someone new in my midst; a partner, a sibling, a cousin of a friend who is "there". I hear stories of people who weren't in touch with their loved ones in months. Whatever opinions one has of the Israeli military campaign in Gaza, we all; including us lefties, have a personal stake in it. I write this as the first push notification I got this morning at 5:30am was from *Ha'aretz* notifying that eight soldiers were killed in combat. There are no words.

And so, that old stereotype of "Arab lovers" is being put to the test in the cruellest way. Many of us know Palestinians in Gaza too, and we are stretched between all these conflicting viewpoints and emotions. Our politics haven't shifted, but suddenly the conflicting demands on our empathy are very immediate. And we need that empathy. The pain and grief of holding our own community is challenged by a simultaneous pain and grief as we are getting more and more horrific news from Gaza and the West Bank.

I was thinking of all this, as on Friday I had spent some hours protesting for the safe return of the hostages. Many people who were there with me were faces I had seen often in anti-occupation demonstrations throughout the years. In other such events I had seen the community come together. One of my friends said to me, right now we need to do everything. We need to campaign for a ceasefire and then to return the hostages and also to oust Netanyahu. You can't really pick your battles and especially you can't abandon your own community.

I'm glad to say that the people closest to me are people able to hold both these things together; who don't feel they have to forgo pain for one community in order to campaign for the safety of another. Who don't fall into self-hatred or righteousness. I am lucky to be surrounded by smart, compassionate people who share my politics and with whom I can grieve. We attend anti-war demonstrations and funerals and shivas together. We comfort our friends while being angry at our government. And we show ourselves, our community and the world, that the human heart can expand and hold empathy for more than one cause, or people.

On the way back from the action Friday I saw graffiti nearby, which seems to embody it all for me, at this moment: "empathy is infinite, there is enough for innocents of all sides". I have never been prouder to be part of a community that can hold empathy and humanity for all innocent lives and is working out of sheer pain and wish to change society around us, rather than enraged righteousness or self-hatred. We may be "Arab lovers", but we hold on to ourselves when we need us the most.

27.12.2023

Discussed: You, me and the next war

Yesterday I went to see Batsheva Dance Company perform 2019. I had seen the work several times; it is truly like nothing else I had seen, including other works by Ohad Naharin. First, the audience enters the studio/theatre from two different entrances and a sheet divides the stage when the work starts. The sheet quickly comes down, and the dancers perform on a sort of catwalk between the two sides of audience members. I had bought a seat in the first row, and the work, which is anyway very visceral, felt very close and immediate. The dancers move a very short distance from the audience, there's a feeling of vulnerability in that, succumbing to the kindness of strangers, literally. The work deals with the heavy price of collectivism and conformity within Israeli society, as some popular songs and games from quintessentially Israeli culture are centred. The audience yesterday was a bit unhinged and joined in the singing; we all needed the collective, even when we felt the price was performed before us: a price of silencing, of fear, and of conformism that costs us in our lives.

At some point of the performance the dancers move to the audience members, take blankets from under the seats and lay on several audience members. The feeling of trust is incredible. They trust in us not to harm them, to hold them. In the background a new version of "you, me and the next war" is recited; this is a text by Hanoch Levin which talks about the ever-present war within Israeli society. He wrote it in 1968, when Israeli society was intoxicated with its triumph in the Six Days War, but some people like him saw the price it would cost in the long run to consolidate occupation over civilian population, and generally conceding to militarism. 2019 was premiered in 2019 (surprise!), but it feels ever-present and ever-timely. When this text was recited, including a horrific line about the knock on the door that everyone in Israel fears (this means for those whose partners or family members are serving in reserve duty, an announcement from the army that they are dead). This felt so horrific and poignant.

On my lap lay the wonderful dancer Iyar Elezra. She is an iconic Batsheva dancer who had returned to the company at the age of thirty-six after having two children. I should say, in parentheses, that I take Gaga classes with many of the dancers who performed, and it was nice to recognise each other from such a short distance. Iyar is also a very talented Gaga teacher whose classes I adore. In fact, she is such a personality and presence that a dance critic I know named her daughter for her.

Since 7th October, via social media, I had learnt that Elezra's husband's cousin was one of the hostages kidnapped to Gaza. Although I don't know her personally, I followed her story via social media, and then her return during the ceasefire. And so, looking at Elezra's head laying quietly on my lap as a dark voice spoke about "you, me and the next war" in which only a photo remains as presence felt really powerful.


Christmas is now over, and I had been thinking about the international responses as well as those from here to the ongoing attacks in Gaza and the fact that there is no viable scenario for returning the hostages. Palestinians live with the knowledge that the world doesn't really care about them, in any substantial way. Netanyahu has been speaking openly about the fact that he is considering "wilful transfer" (read: ethnic cleansing) of Palestinians from Gaza to other countries. This has gone under the radar, maybe because of the timing, while the world is drenched in Christmas celebrations.

In a way, this Christmas has given us, Israelis, a view into what

Palestinians are facing all their lives, and that the world, by and large, doesn't care about us either. True, Israel still enjoys far greater support than any Palestinian leadership, but even for us, the idea that more than a hundred people are still held captive in Gaza and the world continues to turn with little interest in them (and us) is shocking. And so, we have joined, on a smaller scale and momentarily, the dehumanisation that Palestinians have learnt to live with as their reality.

I have been intentionally going to see a lot of Israeli dance since the war broke out. Part of it is as a solidarity action. I feel the need to support the local dance community, especially as many international engagements have been cancelled after the war broke out. For me, dance is a place from which to draw strength. Israeli dance is something that I unequivocally proud of, that I love and makes my heart sing, even in the darkest of times.

After watching 2019 I thought about the fact that the world's response (or non-response) as time passes and the war becomes our reality has taught us both, Israelis and Palestinians, a valuable lesson. International solidarity is important but at the end of the day we will need, all of us, Israelis and Palestinians, to look each other internally, within our societies as well as each other, Palestinian and Israeli societies, in the eye and work to mend what has been so deeply broken here. In the end, we're all stuck here, together. There's something about the intensely Israeli movement language of Ohad Naharin that makes me feel hopeful, even in this dark times; James Baldwin wrote "Not everything that is faced can be changed, but nothing can be changed until it is faced". Israeli dance helps me face the world here. We are facing the worst of us right now. We will need to do the hard work of reckoning in all our societies from within. It will require patience, forgiveness, and kindness. We will need to think about Education as a long arc, rather than an immediate demand. Rebuilding, reconfiguring, defending and protecting in the process. This will require us to stop demanding perfect answers and let people go through processes. It will require us to understand why some people hate us, in the same way that we understand why some people around us hate others, sometimes in our name. But as first step we need to rid ourselves from this deadly, genocidal Israeli leadership that is stopping at nothing, sacrificing countless Palestinian lives and a growing number of Israeli lives too, and to start rebuilding. A place that has given us Naharin and Levin can do that, I know. And there's no time like the present to start, to stop the next war, for you and me.

31.12.2023

## On the start of the academic year and the eve of 2024: a personal note about leaving academia to work full time in politics in Israel–Palestine

Yesterday I went, as every Saturday, to a demonstration calling for a ceasefire and to safeguard human rights in Gaza, and then to a demonstration to bring back hostages. The political climate here is such that these demonstrations are hosted separately. Still, both are important to me

I met up with a feminist legal friend. I had followed her work for a long time, especially about the consequences of the judicial overhaul for women. Just before the war broke out I had attended a lecture she gave in NYU when I was in town. We had kept in touch and corresponded since 7th October, but yesterday was the first time we had met since the war broke out. The last time I had seen her was listening to her speak on Washington Square.

After many delays, the academic year starts in Israeli academic institutions tomorrow. A large part of the student body as well as teaching staff is still on reserve duty, so there will be a break in the semester when the war ends (when will that be?) to let them catch up on the material they had missed. All classes are recorded. There are many similar stories about the Yom Kippur war and events unfolding after it. I never thought I'd live to see a recurrence of this. Sadness has no end.

Today is also New Year's Eve and I thought this juxtaposition is helpful to pause and write more personally about what brought me back here, nearly three years ago. This is also an open invitation if you're an academic thinking of this change, or your students are, or anyone you know is, I'm always happy to chat through my path.

I had lived in Oxford for thirteen years (DPhil and teaching) and one year in NYC. Overall, I was very happy. My career was going OK; I didn't have tenure but felt it wasn't outside my reach. By the time I turned thirty-nine I had published three books; it wasn't a big plan to publish a lot, but my books were a product of happy coincidences and immense privilege.

I learnt early on in my DPhil that I needed to write and find a place that I was able to do so. Writing, for me, is not a choice or a hobby or something I do "when I have time" (I am writing to you today at 5:45am, before a day full of deadlines). I discovered during my academic training that writing fulfilled something very deep for me, and once I found it, I couldn't let it go. Many people around me complained about writer's block and suffering while writing; I loved working on my PhD and books after. It was hard work, yes; I never had sabbaticals and always juggled different things but it was a place I found that became a sanctuary, something that was mine but also to share with others.

I loved teaching, too. The Oxford papers were heavy and repetitive, but I loved them, especially the history of political thought. I loved getting to know young people and being surprised by them every term anew. After I left Oxford I taught at Brookes University in a few departments, then University of Amsterdam and Vrije Universiteit. I enjoyed getting to know different cultures and different styles of teaching to the Oxford style.

This is to say, I didn't dislike academia, and had been doing reasonably well in it. I wasn't disillusioned or frustrated in particular. After a while I got a bit tired from constantly looking for work, but I was incredibly lucky and from the day I stepped into my DPhil program at Oxford I was never unemployed.

Which is a long way to say I liked academia and academia seemed to have liked me well enough.

With time, I had felt the pull to come home strengthen within me. My father became very unwell, then died. I was stuck in Oxford, alone, during the COVID lockdowns, and missed my family a lot. But I also missed my home. The place in which he brought me up and in which I could grieve for him properly. I started coming back for lengthy holidays which included two weeks quarantines in Airbnb in Tel Aviv (remember those days?)

and found I was happier than I had ever been in my pretty flat in Oxford with my good jobs and nicely-put-together life that all my Israeli friends seemed to envy.

I was always involved in politics here in Israel–Palestine. I went to demonstrations whenever I was around. When the big "Balfour protest" (named for the street in which Netanyahu lived) movement started against Netanyahu in the summer of 2020 I went to every one I could. It was amazing. I felt proud to be part of this dissenting part of Israeli society. In parallel, I got to know many people who had worked in the NGO sector here and whose work I followed online. Emails and requests for coffee in exchange for using my position to talk about their work to an international audience were met with enthusiasm and generosity. And so, without knowing, I got to know many of my future colleagues.

But I never sat and thought, ah, this is something I'd like to do. This is the next step for me.

In March 2021 my third book, on dance and activism, was published. On the day of publication, I saw a job advertisement for international director in Peace Now. I had met and chatted with comrades at Peace Now, the movement that educated me in the 1990s. I didn't think deeply of it. I wrote informally to the person who was leaving and to the director and said I was applying. They said, "go for it". I went through two interviews on Zoom. I had some background in fundraising but not in international advocacy. The second interview was on the 5th March 2021, which was also Rosa Luxemburg's 150th birthday. I had five Zooms planned to speak about her life and legacy. The last job interview for Peace Now was 8am UK time, and then it was Rosa till 22:30pm.

I didn't tell any of my friends I was applying until I passed the first interview. I didn't tell my mother either; I knew it would have broken her heart had I not got the job as it was not a plan to come back, but an impulsive decision with no Plan B. I took long walks around my beautiful Oxford flat and tried to imagine what life would look like if I got the job. I had no mental image, but I knew I really wanted it to happen. It just felt right.

I had considered returning to academia here but with political developments being as they were; the deepening of apartheid and occupation alongside an unprecedented surge of protest meant I wouldn't find the real reason I had wanted to return had I come here to be an academic. I will say that there are many incredible lefty academics here who find time for anti-occupation and human rights work as well as academia.

But the trajectory was right. I wanted to work full time in something that was on my mind and around me.

I got the Peace Now job and a week later, with three suitcases, returned to Israel–Palestine after those thirteen years of absence. I still feel it was the best decision I made in my life, though living in the UK taught me a lot too, so I don't regret that either.

It will be three years this March since this all unfolded, so it's helpful to take stock of what are the gains, challenges and struggles I find.

I always felt very deeply that I am privileged and obligated to give back to the community which raised me. I see myself as coming from the wrong side of history. I loved academia but after a while it felt to me too self-focused and at times self-indulgent. I ticked many boxes but something was missing. Also, neo-liberalism in the UK had made the atmosphere unpleasant and the outlook for the future was worse. I wanted to work in a place that had a community, where people work together for a common cause. I have found that. I have found the decentralising of the "I" very refreshing and helpful. Writing for other people's use, speaking on behalf of my comrades, putting my skills into something bigger than my academic CV felt very fulfilling. By the time I had got back I felt I had my share of publications and academic lectures. I didn't feel I need to have to push myself all the time the way that academic job markets demanded of me. It felt good to see my work bear fruit for other people, and more deeply for the cause in which I believe.

The community of people I work with is by far the best community I have ever had. There is true solidarity and people are generous and funny and kind and sophisticated and clever and teach me a lot, every day. Of course, it's not always rainbows and unicorns, I had some tough personal relationships which ended badly here in the NGO sector; some people are really good at talking about Palestinian human rights, not so much in caring for their fellow workers' human rights. But overall, I have found my people.

If you get to know a cause that troubles you and it penetrates your soul you become preoccupied with it. I don't think guilt is a productive feeling for politics, but I feel at least I'm *trying* to do something about a cause I care about deeply. I have been part of some small yet important changes. I formed relationships I couldn't have formed elsewhere.

This sounds really grand, but if something like this burns within you, the drive to change the world in the corner that troubles you, you can't repress it. I don't think I could ever be happy doing something that does not attempt directly to create change in the world. I know most people aren't innately activists in the same way and that's fine; I don't think this is a particularly positive trait. It is just part of who I am, and I felt, after fighting this urge for a long time, I needed to try out and live it to the full. I will say that my close friends and family weren't surprised at my career turn, which means that people who knew me better than myself knew it was coming somehow.

Now, for the challenges.

First and maybe obvious for you, and for me less so, this is a thankless job in which the chances of seeing success in my lifetime are not great. I used to joke and say "I went back home to make peace in Israel–Palestine". Deep down I had hoped I would see it. The more I got to know the depths of occupation and apartheid the less I felt I'd live to see it. This is putting all my energies and everyday work to something I am never likely to see.

Secondly, most personally this change, and at that stage of my life, made me put my ego aside in a profound way. After being an academic for nearly twenty years, I was a novice in a whole new line of work at the age of forty. I had to learn a lot of new things, fast, and I couldn't afford to make mistakes as big matters depended on my work. Any pleasure I had ever had in publishing books, speaking about them, getting positive feedback for my teaching was replaced by having to learn a lot of new things and say openly: I don't know. Help me. This was a deep lesson in humility.

Doing this work means decentralising the "I" all the time. It really is not about me. In any possible way. But the emotional consequences of witnessing wrongs and my complicity in them are vast. The more I got into this work the more I understood why some people are afraid of it. The community is an amazing support but we're all wounded together. Of course, everyone knows it's not about us, and we're not the victims here, yet witnessing one wrong after another, trying everything we know to organise and seeing failures and lack of engagement is a constant challenge.

However, as I wrote, I'm really happy I made this change in my life. This is home, but it will only be home when it is just, when it is actually Israel–Palestine, when there is freedom and protection of human rights for all between the river and the sea. I'll probably never live to see it; who knows how many lives will be lost until we get to a just peace. I am proud to be a small, small part of people who believe this place can be better and don't give up on its people. My comrades are the most humane and optimistic people I've ever worked with, and I'm proud to be part of this small community. Thank you for indulging my self-reflection, if you've read thus far. I wish you and your families a very Happy New Year. If you can afford one wish for us, here, Palestinians and Israelis, it's the end to this horrific war and a year of working towards a political resolution and just peace for all. May 2024 bring some good things to us. We need them.

# JANUARY

The battle and duty to hold on to hope

## Nietzschean inspired New Year's letter: against shame and guilt, for solidarity and responsibility

Happy New Year! Hamas fired a significant missile bombardment exactly at midnight, spurring endless jokes about countdowns. Israel of course continues to attack in Gaza. Tel Aviv felt unusually quiet yesterday; with so many absent, killed, still held hostage, the mood is sombre. Ceasefire couldn't feel further away.

Considering an extraordinary amount of deadlines, I worked and then went to sleep early, woken up by some vague noises. I found myself crying uncontrollably before going to bed; I have not been crying a lot over the past months. Somehow the pain and grief were too heavy to put into tears. But yesterday it all hit home, not least the fact that 7th January is nearly upon us and unless a miracle arrives (please!) we'll be marking three months of this horrific war.

I have been thinking of ideas and praxis I have been trying to commit to and want to take with me into 2024. Bizarrely, perhaps, the inspiration for those recently has been discussing Nietzsche. In the second year of my undergraduate degree, I took a course that made me fall in love with Nietzsche and close readings and taught me a valuable lesson in critical thinking. The course was about the image of the Jew in Nietzsche. The lecturer was a religious Jewish man, Eli Schonfeld, who remains one of the best lecturers I've ever been taught by. We read through several of

Nietzsche's books (mainly *The Birth of Tragedy*, *The Gay Science*, *Beyond Good and Evil*) while tracing the changes in the weight and significance Nietzsche gives Jews in his writings, but beyond that, his critique of Judeo-Christian civilization. I had never felt so immersed in a text and learnt more new ideas in that semester than I had in all political science introductory courses put together. Most significantly, I think, I learnt to separate ideas from biography, to trace changes in conceptual analysis, and to love reading Nietzsche. I had taught some Nietzsche as a teaching assistant in Tel Aviv University, mainly *The Gay Science*. Then when arriving at Oxford, Bonnie Honig was there on sabbatical and I started a conversation with her. In her first book she used Nietzsche in radical democratic theory (which, in essence, is a strand of political theory which seeks to expand the number of speaking voices excluded in the demos; and the theoretical world in which I have been writing since). I spent one semester working under Honig at Northwestern University. And so, my relationship with Nietzsche continued in one form or another. I ended up writing a chapter on Nietzsche in my DPhil thesis; it was not the strongest of chapters but I felt compelled to write it. I focused on the use of dance imagery vis-a-vis his political commentary, in case you wondered. This is a short summary of my relationship with Nietzsche, if you will.

One thing that has remained with me in all these different intellectual turns with Nietzsche was his scathing (often inconsistent, often violent, often incomprehensible) critique of the Judeo-Christian culture he saw hegemonic in his lifetime. Perhaps I returned to think of him when I saw a British colleague post "death to the West" and wondered just how deep his ideas are taking hold just now; the person who's so eaten by resentment and self-loathing they turn towards their own body, their own culture, in a move of self-destruction. I will not attempt to give an introduction to Nietzsche's writing here but suffice to say he was highly critical of shame and guilt as central in Judeo-Christian culture. I'm also butchering his use of this concept, forgive me; I swore I wouldn't transform this essay into a political theory orgy. Perhaps discussing that first course recently together with thinking about guilt and shame have pushed me to make these connections today.

It is very hard not to feel and perform guilt constantly if you're following the news from our little region. The closer you are to Israel/Palestine, and specifically, to someone affected by everything unfolding since 7th October, the more inclined you are to feel guilty, all of the time. Yesterday in my Gaga class the teacher, a very young dancer, said "imagine you are at a party and a beautiful sunrise is coming up". We froze and someone said: "wrong image". He apologised and we continued. Bear in mind all of us Israelis, to varying degrees, carry survivors' guilt. Why were my cousins in the bomb shelter for hours on end while I was far away? Why did some people I know get abducted from their home while I sleep comfortably in my bed? Why are soldiers getting killed daily while I go to the supermarket, to dance class, to meet with friends? Sometimes the guilt is less bearable than others.

If you are an Israeli who intentionally follows news from Gaza (Israeli media still doesn't show the effects of Israel's attack on Gaza), or, even, the horrors unfolding on the West Bank; from expedited ethnic cleansing to forcible transfer to administrative arrests, the list goes on; guilt has a dual facet. Not only am I surviving other people around me by pure chance, but horrible, horrific things are being done in my name. If this preoccupies you it's hard to get on with anything one needs to get done, even if it's for the struggle.

Another emotion or feeling (conscious or self-conscious) that we Israelis entrenched in the struggle against occupation and apartheid experience all the time is shame. The word "shame" is often chanted in demonstrations here, yet our leaders seem to be shameless. And the more evidence we see coming out of Gaza; violence incurred by soldiers, humiliation for the sake of it (an image circulated widely in Israel was of "Hamas militants" sitting in their underwear, blindfolded, guarded by Israeli soldiers) the more overcome by shame one feels. We hear more and more of abductions, of vandalism, of ruin for the sake of it. Of course, it's not the entire army, yet when these pieces of evidence emerge it's hard not to be ruined with shame.

Both guilt and shame, Nietzsche had taught me, are not generative sentiments. Years in organising taught me that if you want people to listen to you, calling them, collectively, war criminals, immoral and wretched won't bring them to you. Of course, maybe you don't want to engage with the collective from which these actions emerge, which is fine; but if you do wish to engage the community you wish to change, inflicting shame or guilt isn't likely to make people come out to your demonstration.

Moreover, and this is something I am learning more and more, deepening your own process with these feelings and emotions must be internal rather than externalised, especially not to your Palestinian comrades. When the death toll in Gaza is over 30,000 people it would be wrong to ask Palestinian friends to hold my guilt and shame and help me move through them. It would be inflicting upon them more harm that my community is anyway enacting on them. Generally, I think, dealing with this is quite an individual journey, as we all feel guilt and shame about different things. But, visiting your crisis isn't likely to help another person; if anything, it would add more guilt or shame to their burden. And again, from an organising point of view, shame and guilt aren't galvanising for action.

So, a challenge I've been working through myself and would like to share with you today is transforming guilt and shame into solidarity and responsibility (or interchangeably, or in a mix of all those). In my third book I wrote quite a lot about solidarity, but I still can't define it accurately; I think in the most fundamental way it is the ability to decentralise the "I" as a motor for action, to detach myself, my feelings, my emotions and vulnerabilities from the action I think should be done. First and foremost, it entails the ability to analyse who is most hit by the policy I wish to change, or the action I wish to reverse, and consequently which are the forces that need to be mobilised in order to create that change. It might mean that I, my feelings and their consequences won't be centre stage; in fact, usually that's the case. When it comes to structural power analysis this becomes even more key. In organising with Palestinian comrades, it is the case that we, Israelis, have advantage in power structures and in working in our communities. However, to get most traction or to centralise voices that must be heard we can't occupy (pun intended) central decision-making, organising and galvanising positions. With time and experience I've learnt that some things should not be done by us, or at least not *on behalf* of Palestinian voices. My voice is always mobilised within my own community; Israelis who feel connection to this place and want it to be better. But here solidarity action gets complex yet this analysis is essential.

Dealing with guilt, specifically, is more of a challenge. Not only are we conditioned to be mobilised by it but it is, especially at this time, impossible to do away with. I find thinking about responsibility here helpful. My taxes are paying for a policy which I grossly oppose. I am taking every opportunity I can to speak up against it. But I am not responsible for every single thing an Israeli soldier is doing in Gaza, in the same way that all Gazans aren't responsible for Hamas's actions. We bear collective responsibility in sustaining structures of which we are part, so we should continue to analyse them and see how we can change them. Again, more often than not, this entails decentralising the "I". Where am I entrenched and what is my power in the circles in which I move? What are the discourses that resonate with me where I can interleave my voice? Not to galvanise change, alone, or even in a small group, but as systemic rupture that enables more voices to be heard and my own voice, as coming from the wrong side of history, to be less central. Perhaps paradoxically, then, and contrary to what we are brought up with in our cultures, making the change from our position, as Jewish Israelis, means at once being embedded in our societies while decentralising ourselves within them. These are dual concentric motions which happen all the time at once; we cannot exclude ourselves from our collectives, nor can we continue to take a too central place within them.

So, I am making conscious attempts to dance away from guilt and shame towards solidarity and responsibility, to shy away from the extreme enactments of resentment in shame and guilt and to move to collective structures that can create change in the world. I started with Nietzsche (but not very deeply, sorry Friedrich) and I will end on one of my favourite quotations from his work, maybe because I ended 2023 in dance, a ballet class, and will start 2024 in the same way. But perhaps because part of my internal discipline, before and during this war, was to hold contradictions yet open up possibilities for rupture: "One must still have chaos in oneself to be able to give birth to a dancing star", from *Thus Spoke Zarathustra*.

03.01.2024

Discussed: The battle and duty to
hold on to hope

January is a deadline-heavy month, and so I find myself escaping into work, which is helpful to an extent. But not really, as my work is politics. But it's a privilege, of course. I find the biggest battle in my mind and heart these days is trying to hold on to hope.

On a very basic level, I feel that I do not have the privilege to despair. I see myself as writing and acting from the wrong side of history, and so I don't have the luxury of sitting pretty and doing nothing. But, holding axioms like these doesn't necessarily translate into emotional realities.

I find the periods of time I can go through without thinking of Gaza are becoming shorter. If at first, I could draw on images I saw on Twitter and Instagram and push myself to think of life there, but the more devastation I see and the more gory images are coming through, I realise I really cannot imagine life there, and probably none of us can.

Yesterday the Israeli army killed a high-ranking Hamas official in Lebanon, something that will upset both Hamas in Gaza and Hezbollah in Lebanon. I am old enough to remember the second Lebanon war, and the withdrawal from Lebanon, and my political education comes from Peace Now which was founded in part as a response to fighting there. So, words of trepidation I hear in the media about fear of the Lebanese scene warming up resonate very deeply.

Indeed, for months now residents have been evacuated from the north of Israel because of the hefty barrage of missile bombardment from Hezbollah. It was said that another hostage deal, that was on the cards and in discussions, was pushed away due to this assassination. Whereas all eyes are on Gaza for geopolitical reasons, the Lebanese border has been explosive for a long time. Having served in the army up north I love that area; it is so beautiful and picturesque. One of the special things about Israel–Palestine broadly is that you have a desert and a Swiss-looking forest within an hour's drive of each other. I can't stop thinking of the people who have been displaced from the border, friends, family of friends, those places I visited so often now ruined by missile bombardment.

We are nearing the 7th January, three months of devastation and ruin. We have fallen into a routine of despair with little spirals downwards. Yesterday my mother's retirement home asked her to secure her flat as they are afraid of attacks from the north. A friend texted me last weekend; it was his first break from reserve duty in Gaza since 7th October. "How are you?" I asked. "I don't know," he answered. I know him from mutual work in the Israeli left civil society. I can't imagine what he must feel like.

I ran into another friend who looked exhausted. She's been solo parenting since the 7th with her partner in reserve duty. Three young children, running to the bomb shelter, having to work during it all. I remember everyone's breakdown over childcare during COVID. Now we're living through a similar crisis but without the ability to vent about it as those left behind.

In Israel those who have been evacuated since 7th October are becoming desperate. I have heard of violence breaking out in hotels that house them. There is also a quiet epidemic of suicide in Israeli society; among those who have been evacuated, among those who have been involved in one way or another. Survivors of the 7th October. I'm hearing quietly of more and more cases.

Last week, a traumatised soldier who had a short break from his duty in Gaza shot three of his friends, who were lightly injured. The popular Israeli satire TV show "It's a Wonderful Country" had a hard-hitting sketch about a traumatised soldier who sits, disengaged, while his family argues about politics. "I'm going back to Gaza," he says at the end of the sketch. "It's easier there". The actor who plays the soldier has been explicit about his own trauma. It's a strong statement.

I find the need to hold on to hope, because I can. I am not in Gaza. I am not suffering hunger or diseases. I don't have family there who are fleeing persecution. I don't have family there on reserve duty. I don't have to care for young children while fearing for the life of my loved one. I am not traumatised by war. I have not witnessed unfathomable horrors. The fact that I can contemplate whether I can imagine those horrors or not is testimony of my immense privilege. I have not been evicted from my house. I come from privilege and don't feel the wear of this war on my livelihood.

It is our duty, those of us not on the frontline in one way or another, to hold on to hope, for those who can't afford to do so now. It is our duty to hold on to others' pain so that they can relieve themselves from it for a short hope. It is our duty to acknowledge our luck and privilege, every day, and see what we can gain from that—what we can do for others. It is our duty to remember and remind that humanity knows how to come up from ruins, to mend itself. It is our duty to remember and remind ourselves that we, as human beings, know how to hold each other's grief and pain. That we know how to mend other's broken hearts. We cannot afford our hearts to break. This is what I tell myself every day.

05.01.2024

## Can we actually think about Gaza?

We are coming up to three months of this horrific war. It seems like both yesterday and thirty years ago that it had started. But whereas the dangers and horrors awaiting us were quite expected to those of us following politics in Israel–Palestine, the magnitude, as well as the effect on the ground, have been shocking.

I'll start from the ugly, basic truth. Israel has been attacking Gaza on an almost annual basis; sometimes more than that. Referred internally in army slang as "mowing the lawn", the object of these attacks was to deter Hamas by visiting incalculable human cost on Palestinians in Gaza, causing death and wrecking infrastructure. This has happened often since Israel disengaged from the Gaza Strip, meaning it removed its settlements and military forces, yet kept control of the crossings in and out of the Strip including the marine border, thus maintaining de facto occupation of the Strip.

When Israel started attacking Gaza on the 7th October, this was hardly new, nor surprising. Israel has been doing so for years, and without something as immense and traumatising as the Hamas attacks on the south of Israel occurring to it. Indeed, this is true for all governments and for those from nearly all political sides; the liberal-democratic government that provided a short hiatus from Netanyahu's long reign, entitled "the government of change", had also attacked Gaza in August 2022. And Netanyahu's sitting government is by far the most radical right-wing, Jewish supremacist and overtly racist my homeland has known.

This is a very long way to say the beginning of the Israeli attacks on Gaza were horrifying yet not shocking when they started. When I chose to go and work in advocacy for freedom of movement in Gaza I thought mainly of these attacks and of the circularity by which ordinary citizens in Gaza are paying the price for a skewed power politics between the Israeli government and Hamas. I felt helpless seeing homes ruined, people dying en masse, entire parts of cities and agricultural areas devastated, all in my name.

When I started writing these essays, I kept count of the number of people killed in Gaza, of the devastation incurred on the Strip. Over time I found myself struggling more and more to write about it and moreover to think about it.

If anything, I tried to think about this more; the 7th October is becoming further, we are, in the nature of grief, healing slowly. There is more open discussion of what happened and what didn't happen on the 7th. Some of the hostages returned and shared their experiences. We in Israel are turning our energies towards saving the ones who are still there. The processing will take a long time, especially for those implicated directly; but for most of the Israeli population, life has taken turns since the 7th October. Many of our friends and loved ones are in combat in Gaza. The economy is suffering tremendously. The government has no plan for "the day after the war", and all it issues are statements that endorse genocide and revenge.

Which means we have much more mental space to think about Gaza. And yet actually thinking about Gaza is becoming harder by the day.

It is clear that the death and devastation visited on the Strip by Israeli attacks is unprecedented and impossible to comprehend from a distance. The entire north of the Strip is ruined. The south is becoming internally suffocated by famine, diseases and lack of decent living conditions of any kind. People are dying at rates we cannot comprehend, and in increasingly hideous ways, an hour's drive away from us.

In the past I wrote here about the Arendt interview in which she says that she did not know what happened in the concentration camps. Our life now is the opposite. This is perhaps the most documented genocide in history. For those of us who are following Gazans on social media following events from Gaza is overwhelming and immediate, and unmediated. Hundreds of thousands, nearly millions, of reels and photos of starving children, of rubble burying human corpses or bodies about to become corpses. Of children seeking a way out of this reality. Live footage of bombings. Of soldiers destroying buildings, cultural institutions, artefacts that have survived thousands of years. These are my people, and they are destroying a whole culture. The violence is immense and complete and enacted on all avenues of life. The suffering is incomprehensible. If you follow events on the news you get a mediated version even if it's an independent or radical news source. But the violence is unfolding live for all of us who are watching on social media on various platforms.

And yet, the difficulty of comprehending does not disappear, if anything it is becoming harder. An overflow of visual information, including the need to discern fake news from real which is present both on social media and other forms of media, the images that haunt our feeds, the constant presence of those families escaping, where to? We know they have nowhere to go; all this makes processing of Gaza as a name, a place, a community, a culture, harder not easier to fathom.

I am forcing myself to follow these images, reels, shrieks of pain, running human beings, running from me, running from my people. But it doesn't make it easier to "think" about Gaza. The fact that we are witnessing this unfold live before our eyes does not mean we can understand or deeply internalise what is happening and how it is related to us.

In a strange way, I felt a relief that South Africa is bringing a case against Israel on charges of genocide to the International Court of Justice. All these images will be used as evidence, no doubt; there is also enough first-hand evidence of those who were able to escape Gaza. The definition of genocide is complex, yet it is hard to deny that the totality as well as the intentionality of Israeli attacks on civilian population. This was discussed in a piece in *Local Call/972 magazine* published by Yuval Abraham who revealed on record quotes that the Israeli army continued to attack civilian targets even when it knew civilians were in danger, as well as quotes on record of Israeli politicians calling for genocide and repopulation of the Strip by Jewish settlements. When this attack started, I pleaded for a return to international law and human rights. This is now happening.

But, this does not diminish the challenge of reducing the distance between reality as it unfolds in front of our eyes, representing this reality in our minds and drawing conclusions: political, moral, legal and human for ourselves. Meaning: to think about it. I am finding my internal dialogue silenced in the face of the horrors unfolding in front of me live, overwhelming me with words I cannot find. Yet I cannot afford not to speak, I cannot afford to lose my words. I think it's fair to say that some human horrors transcend what we can express in words, what we can put into a story for ourselves. Some things are just raw pain and violence that transcend our ability to mediate them into a narrative, especially when no end is in sight and when we think things can't get worse, they indeed become that.

So, we can accept that at this moment, we cannot "think" of Gaza. We cannot create a coherent narrative, to put the suffering, the loss, the erasure of a human culture into words. At least not us, observing from outside. There will be many stories and narratives arising out of this moment; some already are emerging. We can forgo our voice and listen. We can accept that some things do not reduce the distance between presentation and representation. That some horrors are unspeakable. We can let go of our human need to represent but still demand to bear witness; to listen to testimonies, to absorb the images.

The word genocide is hard to stomach, especially as a Jewess. But once we start to talk in terms of international law, it is our obligation, as citizens of the world, implicated in this horrific moment in different ways, to listen, to bear witness, to move to due process and accountability. We can and must accept this discrepancy; between our ability as human beings to think about what is happening, to represent horrific events in our psyche, as well as to agree that the only way to get out of this mess is by conforming to international law and human rights.

I continue counting the Palestinian dead, now reaching 30,000, I continue to bear witness. I understand that I cannot think, speak, represent the symbolic, human layer that transcends these facts and figures. I understand that at this moment what is happening in Gaza transcends the human psyche. But the human psyche can also rebuild, reaffirm human rights, reaffirm accountability, reaffirm justice. And so, I force myself to continue bearing witness and hold on to that hope, so that we will be in a different time when all human beings between the river and the sea are free and safe, we can start thinking, together, as equals.

Can we forgive our brother's murderer? (and does it matter for the future of Israel–Palestine?)

I am on my period again. I've stopped counting how many times this has happened during the war. It feels like counting these re-occurrences only makes sense when you are counting towards *something*, the end of the war, a ceasefire.

I have been debating with friends whether we can even still call this a war. There have been consistent attacks on the north of Israel but the attacks on Gaza have become very one-sided. Tel Aviv feels back to its buzzing self, even if a large part of the population is still in reserve duty. It feels both normal and odd. The fact that the academic year finally started was the last step towards declaring the beginning of a routine and that we do not know how long this will last. So it is a sad routine.

My cousins who had been displaced since 7th October are moving to their second temporary home, as a community, somewhere in the centre of Israel. They have not been to their home in the kibbutz in the south for three months. One of my cousins went back so he can work the land there. There are still quite a few missile raids and alarms in the area closest to Gaza in the south of Israel, which is mostly vacant.

It is my mother's eightieth birthday today. We will go to a concert and yesterday I brought her to Sipur Pashut. It was as lovely and uplifting as ever, I was pleased she was able to see the togetherness and love of books that has been my mainstay for so long and of course, we got some birthday books for her.

I am reading Motty Fogel's book *Not a Memoir*. He moves in

my circles, and I had heard his name before the book was published. I got the book at Sipur Pashut when he did a signing for its release. We had a short exchange, and I placed the book on my large to be read pile

My friends have been waxing lyrical about the book and so I started reading it. Fogel was raised in a settlement in the West Bank, became secular and also changed his ideological position. In 2011 his brother, his brother's wife and three of their five children were murdered by a Palestinian in the settlement of Itamar. The twelve-year-old daughter who survived found the bodies, and another sibling who survived, a baby, and called the police when she returned home.

The book is beautiful. First, it is one of the most gentle and dense texts I have read in Hebrew. The book is not about the murder, or the process around it, but rather about reflections on life and especially on reading. Fogel's ability to recount the influence of books he reads, in particular, Georges Perec, is truly extraordinary. I would say wait till it is translated but it will never be as beautiful in translation.

The murder plays a part in the book. Fogel recounts the funeral, the shiva, the night in which he got the phone call announcing the murder of his younger brother and family. What it means to be a "brother". How his family changed after the murder. But this is not the core of the book. The core of the book is without doubt, narration of reading books, including the Bible. As he had come from religious upbringing, he has this beautiful ability to relate Perec, Proust, Tolstoy and others to key segments from the Bible.

What has struck me is the lack of anger in the book. The lack of a wish for revenge. In the chapter I read today (I read a chapter a day, with breakfast) he wrote about revenge. Revenge, Fogel writes, is the wish that the whole world experiences this dramatic stopping of life that he was destined to live with. The feeling of "before and after" and that nothing will ever be the same.

He acknowledges this wish exists, but he does not subscribe to it.

I have been thinking a lot about revenge, and its opposites. I have also been thinking of a paradigm shift that I have been going through these past three months.

In my childhood, during the Oslo days, we thought that if we, Palestinians and Israelis, would "get along" as people, we could get along as peoples. A lot of foreign money and attempts in reconciliation were put into getting Palestinian and Israeli youth in large circles in which we talked. The attempt was to show us how similar we actually were. I was thirteen when I started attending those. I remember being struck mostly by how different we were. I lived with privileges and power that my Palestinian peers could but dream of. We had very little in common. We were thrown into this make-believe theatre in which if me and my Palestinian counterpart both said we liked cats, then hey, we are the same! We both are thirteen-year-old kids who like cats! But the fact that she would have to wait for three hours in a checkpoint and I was the relative of those soldiers who held her in the checkpoint, was pushed aside.

If there is anything significant that came out of these three months is the complete and utter breakdown of the Oslo paradigm. The wish to reproduce some kind of façade of externalised liberal democracy in Palestine, without any substantial power or ability for self-defence. The classic two-state paradigm sees Israel as still holding the monopoly over arms between the river and the sea, which Weber fans will realise still makes us Israelis de facto the sovereign. Nour Odeh, a Palestinian journalist and commentator I highly appreciate, who has held public offices in the Palestinian Authority, wrote astutely on Twitter that in the end, if we grant Palestinians the right to self-determination this means we cannot veto what they choose.

I feel the collapse of Oslo is occurring in tandem with the crisis of modern–liberal democracies around the world; the sway of English speaking countries towards authoritarian regimes (Trump 2024? and UK post-Brexit), the crises in the EU and inability to curb right-wing leaders within it, and of course the strengthening of China, India and Russia on the world stage).

So, if there is one thing we know it's that replicating some kind of make-believe American model of democracy elsewhere won't work. We will have to work out here how to govern ourselves, each people for themselves, and it will probably not be Westernised liberal democracy. That is not necessarily a bad thing.

But the other thing I am thinking about is that how we, Israelis and Palestinians, live together, does not have to be governed by models of "co-existence". We need a political arrangement, most likely with some international supervision at first, ensured by legal provisos and securities. We need to be able to live our lives without fearing each other. Palestinians who had been living under occupation for so long cannot be demanded to reconcile with Israelis on a personal level. I know and have accepted that for many of my Palestinian peers, especially in the West Bank and Gaza, and in a different way, in East Jerusalem, I am no different to the soldier who keeps them at the checkpoint, still, thirty years after Oslo; or at worst, the soldier who looks on when they live with settler violence as a daily routine. I am one and the same with the government that takes their land away, bit by bit. In a way they are right. In a similar vein, I understand well that for the many families who are grieving the loss of their loved ones on the Israeli side, and despite the dramatic power discrepancies between us, the weight of grief on Israelis is immense, there will always be that life-changing event that cannot be discredited and changes how you see the Palestinian side.

Many of the people affected by 7th October directly had called for a political resolution. Political resolution had been seen as the opposite of the Israeli government policy of revenge, which is at best, the continuation of the war for an indefinite period of time without focus, and at worst, incessant and indiscriminate attacks amounting to genocide. But here I do not think the opposite of revenge is forgiveness but rather a political resolution. Not the ability to sit in a room with your brother's killer and say, "I forgive you", or to write that in your book, but the ability to live your life without fearing the next murder. There is an arrangement in place that protects us, both, and takes into account the power disparities between us without glossing over them.

Perhaps one of the most dehumanising tropes towards Palestinians and Israelis is this assumption that one side is all bad, one side is all good, we will learn to get along personally, and then peace will come.

I have Palestinian friends I adore. I can talk to them frankly and they can talk to me. I have known Palestinians I cannot stand. Does this mean peace will never come to the Middle East? Well, no, because there are also Israelis I cannot stand, and there are

Israelis I adore, who are my friends and comrades. None of us are all good and none of us are all bad. The move to "love the player, hate the game" (forgive the crude wording) is that we do not essentialise about collective dynamics and power structures from interpersonal relationships, "love thy neighbour", and we can critique power structures without seeing deductive reasoning asking us to relate to individuals. We can get on as human beings, or not; because we know there are structures in place to govern how we behave as collectives not harming each other.

So, I do not want to ask my cousins whether they forgive those Hamas militants who displaced them for three months and by pure chance did not cost them their life. I do not feel compelled to ask Fogel whether he forgave his brother's murderer. Perhaps he cannot, and that is fine. These do not matter because in the end, if we have structures in place to ensure that these events will not happen again, our relationship as individuals will not matter. And, with time, when we stop fearing each other daily, perhaps more personal relationships will develop, but even if not, we will live here together as equals, governing ourselves as we see right, with the structural imbalances between us rectified. We do not need to live as brothers and sisters, not even as friends. We just need to live together as not always potential murderers.

Fogel quotes a lot from the story of Cain and Abel, and I say: I am not my brother's keeper, and I am not my sister's keeper. We just need an arrangement to be that keeper so that this story does not occur here, ad infinitum.

Shabbat shalom, a Saturday of peace.

# About the Authors

Dana Mills is a writer, dancer, and peace and human rights advocate. She received her DPhil from the University of Oxford in 2014. As an academic, she has held posts, among other institutions, in the University of Oxford, NYU, Northwestern University, American Dance Festival, Martha Graham School of Contemporary Dance, University of Amsterdam and the Hannah Arendt Center at Bard College. Since 2021 she has been working in Israeli–Palestinian civil society on a variety of issues. Mills has written many articles and three books: *Dance and Politics: Moving beyond Boundaries* (MUP, 2016); the biography *Rosa Luxemburg* (Reaktion, 2020) and *Dance and Activism: a century of radical dance across the world* (Bloomsbury, 2021).

Sally Abed is a Palestinian socialist and feminist living in the mixed city of Haifa. She is in the national leadership of Standing Together, the largest Arab-Jewish grassroots movement in Israel.